BUILD
YOUR LIFE
TO INSPIRE

BUILD YOUR LIFE TO INSPIRE

TRANSFORM YOUR LIFE IN 50 DAYS
AND START LIVING THE LIFE YOU WANT

RUDOLF BRENYAH

ISBN 978-1-5272-9152-2

www.rudolfbrenyah.com

TABLE OF CONTENTS

ACKNOWLEDGEMENTS

To my loving mother, Felicia Adjei, who kept reminding me from a young age that one day I will be great, and nicknamed me 'International'. Speaking into existence that one day her son will be influential internationally.

To my family and close friends, who have supported and prayed for me.

To the nation of Ghana, may this book help us continue to be a nation that is committed to excellence. I believe in us!

To all the people of the developing nations, the so-called 'third world countries', who at times have been conditioned to believe that they cannot be all that they were created to be. May this book change this narrative for you.

To Alfred Batler, who started off as my youth leader and later became a big brother and a mentor, but sadly passed away in October 2018.

To every individual, who has a desire to be great and significant, you can achieve this in your life. I believe in you!

INTRODUCTION

You probably picked up this book because you are tired of living a mediocre life, and have no intention to come here just to make up numbers, being part of a statistic. Perhaps, you are tired of not being celebrated for your uniqueness. On your way to school or work, you tell yourself, 'There is so much more I can offer to the world than what I am currently doing'. Do you know you what? You are right. There is more that you can offer the world, but, like most people in the world, you probably don't know how and where to start from.

There are guidelines that can help you get where you desire to be in life. I have studied successful people in all walks of life, and I constantly see common denominators in their journey. I have managed to narrow them down to 10, and I will show them to you in the next 50 days or less, depending on how you decide to read this book, whether as a daily devotional or in one sitting.

It is time for you to truly live the life you want; you owe it to yourself and to the world. The guidelines I share in this book will help you become the best version of yourself, so you can also contribute your excellence to the world. I utilise these principles inspired by the high achievers and successful people I know, and they continue to bring wealth and fulfilment to my life. If these guidelines work for the likes of Oprah Winfrey, Bruce Lee,

Cristiano Ronaldo, and Mark Zuckerberg, just to name a few, then they can work for you too. The people I just named are not any different from you. The only difference is their commitment to the guidelines and steps I am going to share with you in this book.

As it stands today, there are 7.6 billion people on the planet. Not one of these 7.6 billion people came to this planet as an experiment or as a biological mistake. Everyone, including you, arrived here with and for a purpose. We all have one thing in common called 'potential,' and we are all looking for personal fulfilment. The above statement is my conviction in life. It is the reason why I became an inspirational speaker and why I wrote this book for you.

The average human being lives their life as an experiment; they are not sure how to become the best version of themselves— maybe this describes you. Do you believe that greatness can only be achieved by a select few? Can you confidently say that you are not experimenting with your life, and know exactly what you want? Do you know how to get there? The gap between what you want and how to get there is what this book will help you with. You cannot afford to wait any longer. Decide today to become the best version of yourself. It is high time you stepped up to the plate: let the world see your uniqueness, and make a difference while you are here. If you want to achieve greatness in your life, then let us begin right now as you flip the page and read on.

DAY 1

TOPIC: **INTRODUCTION**

Self-discovery is the process of knowing who you are, and what you have. It is the first key that unlocks greatness. Several people go through life doing what others expect them to do. They go to school, get a job, and do back-to-back activities. They never really settle down for once to find out who they truly are and what they have. Many of these people are unfulfilled.

Let us look away from others for a moment and focus on you instead. Do you truly know who you are? How do you define yourself? Do you know your gifts and talents? Have you discovered your passion? What are the things that make you happy and give you that sense of fulfilment?

Self-discovery is a lifetime journey of accessing your inner self to know who you are, your abilities, purpose, and core values that guide you in life. This trip begins with self-awareness, and proceeds to an exploration of personal interests, as well as future dreams and hopes. The journey culminates in self-knowledge, which guides you towards experiences and situations that will help you thrive. Self-discovery is an essential part of personal and professional growth.

Anyone who prospered in this world discovered themselves first. From Bill Gates, to Mark Zuckerberg, Oprah Winfrey, Michael Jordan, Warren Buffet, among others. It was Oprah Winfrey who said, 'I was once afraid of people saying "Who does she think she is?" Now I have the courage to stand and say, "This is who I am"'.

Oprah Winfrey was born to a low-income mother, who was a teenager at the time of her birth. For this reason, her early life was anything but luxurious. She started experiencing sexual abuse at 9, got pregnant at 14, and gave birth to a child that died shortly after birth. Even when she began working at a local television station after completing her university education, the producer sacked her because he found her to be unfit for television. However, because she had already discovered herself, none of these things could stop her. She took on another show in Chicago, and the rest is history.

You can hardly go far in life without self-discovery. If you do not know who you are, other people will give you an identity. In the next few days, we will dig deeper into self-discovery. I am optimistic that by the end of this sub-theme, you would have discovered yourself, thereby receiving the first key that opens the door of greatness.

'Discovering who you are today is the first step to being who you will be tomorrow'.

Destiny's Odyssey

DAY 2

SUB-THEME: **SELF-DISCOVERY**

TOPIC: **BENEFITS OF SELF-DISCOVERY**

One of the benefits of self-discovery is improved decision-making. It is common knowledge that decisions determine destiny. If you seek a great destiny, then you must make great decisions. One of the foundational blocks of making great decisions is self-discovery. When you are aware of who you are and what you have, you can make choices that align with your true self, leading to a happier and more satisfied life experience. We are saddled with the responsibility of choosing from life's multitude of options every day, and our choices not only reflect what we know about ourselves, but also determine what life does with us.

Another advantage of self-discovery is that it will give you a sense of value and significance that every human being craves. This desire to feel valuable is the reason why, at times, people spend huge amounts of money on designer clothes and shoes—they believe that their value will come from wearing luxury designer brands. Clothes and shoes do not make you significant or valuable.

When you discover yourself, you will know that it is you who makes the clothes and shoes valuable. The other day, I was reading about the Air Force One plane, and discovered that it has more to do with the type of passenger on board, than with the plane model itself. Anytime the U.S. president is a passenger on any plane, it automatically becomes an Air Force One plane. It is the value of the president that changes the name of a plane. The same applies to you once you discover yourself; it is you that will add value to any environment. If people do not discover themselves, they tend to act out of character in order to feel valuable and significant; this is when people will do anything for a moment of clout. Instead of selling yourself short in return for recognition, be determined to discover why you are here and what kind of contribution you can make to the world, and you will, by default, be significant and valuable.

Self-discovery gives you a boost in self-esteem and confidence. When you discover why you are here, and what kind of contribution you can make to the world, it will increase your confidence and self-esteem. It will destroy that mindset of 'I am here, just to make up numbers', and you will adopt the mindset of 'I am here with and for a purpose, and the world must experience the real me before I leave the earth'. If you are struggling with low self-esteem because you are comparing your life to others', you have failed to see the value in yourself, and you are putting others on a pedestal. Once you discover yourself and you go after your goals in life, you will have more respect for yourself, and begin to like yourself more; this will boost your confidence and self-esteem.

Self-discovery increases productivity. When you are working on a project that aligns with your true self, your mind and body engage fully with it, thereby releasing enough strength for you to get the work done. However, when you undertake a job that does not align with your authentic self, you will struggle with meeting deadlines. Besides, people are generally more creative when they do something that aligns with their natural abilities. Self-discovery helps you know what your true passion is and to choose jobs that align with that passion.

Self-discovery is the first step to achieving the life you truly desire. The truth is that your desires will remain with you, whether you know them or not; and you will remain unhappy if you do not fulfil them. But there's no way you can achieve these dreams without being aware of them. Therefore, you must discover yourself.

> 'The greatest discovery in life is self-discovery. Until you find yourself you will always be someone else. Become yourself'.
>
> *Myles Munroe*

DAY 3

SUB-THEME: **DISCOVER YOURSELF**

TOPIC: **COMMON OBSTACLES TO SELF-DISCOVERY**

Just like any other important entity in life, there are things that hinder people from engaging in self-discovery. I have discovered that nothing worth having comes easy. In other words, there will be obstacles to achieving whatever will truly benefit your life, and if you are not aware of those hindrances, it will be difficult to overcome them. Therefore, today, we will consider the common obstacles to self-discovery.

One of the obstacles to self-discovery is fear. Some people have painted a picture that is not true to themselves, hence they are afraid of finding out who they truly are. Others are afraid that they might find things about themselves that they do not like, thereby labelling themselves as worthless or useless. To avoid the pain of this realisation, they prefer not to engage in self-discovery. However, when you refuse to truly discover yourself, you limiting the level of success and joy you could have had in life.

Another obstacle to self-discovery is inadequate self-love. Many people are not taught to love themselves; as such, they do not care about discovering who they really are. If you grew up with criticism rather than encouragement, you will most likely crave social acceptance. Therefore, you are more likely to pick up the traits, ideas, and attitudes of others than find out who you truly are and stand up for yourself.

Also, society has taught a lot of people that it is not profitable to engage in self-discovery. For example, your parents probably wanted you to study medicine and surgery, engineering, or banking and finance at university even if your passion lies in the creative arts. They believe that you can make a living with a degree in any of the former courses than the latter. Therefore, you do not even try to determine what you truly desire.

Furthermore, some people are too busy to discover themselves. They are always engaging in one activity or the other. They have deadlines to meet every other day, and cannot take the time out to truly look into their inner selves. They do not create time for self-reflection; as such, they do not become aware of their true self. The truth is that, whether now or later, everyone will get to know who they really are regardless. The only difference is that those who discover themselves early and follow the guidance of their real self will live a fulfilled, happy life, while those who do so when it is too late will live with regrets. You have a choice!

'Knowing yourself is the beginning of all wisdom'.

Aristotle

DAY 4

SUB-THEME: DISCOVER YOURSELF

TOPIC: HOW TO DISCOVER YOURSELF

Self-discovery has two major parts, knowing who you are, and knowing what you have. These two parts are interrelated, but for the sake of clarity, we will separate them.

To discover who you are, you have to change your perception about yourself. Put differently, you need to begin to think of yourself in a good light. Medical science tells us that about 200 million sperm cells are released when a man meets his wife. Of all these, only one gets to the egg; and that one was you. You were never a mistake; you are important. You deserve to know who you truly are. You have the right to follow your true dreams and passions. You are not less human than any other person regardless of their status or background. You truly deserve the joy and peace that comes from self-discovery.

Furthermore, to discover yourself, find out what you are capable of doing with your life. As I mentioned earlier, if you do not know yourself, you will think that you are here just to make up numbers. Therefore, you must answer the following questions, 'Why am I here?' and 'What can I do?' Once you can clarify and answer these two questions, you are starting to take the right steps towards self-discovery. I remember reading a book by the late Bahamian minister, Dr. Myles Munroe, called *In Pursuit of Purpose*. In that book, he made a profound statement, 'Purpose is only found in the mind of the creator'. I concur with that quote— no one will know a product better than its manufacturer. What helped me discover my true self was finding out what the creator has destined for me by looking at the gifts, talents, and strengths he gave me. I believe that for every creation, there must be a creator. It makes perfect sense that I was created by a higher being known as God; you may refer to him as Yahweh, Allah or the man upstairs. You may not be a man or a woman of faith, but I want us to look at a quote that helped me discover myself. We will only look at the first line of the passage found in the first book of the bible Genesis 1:26. 'And God said, let us make man in our image, after our likeness…' When I read this quote, it boosted my self-esteem and confidence. I said to myself, *There is no way I am here only to make up numbers if I was created in the image and likeness of God.* The same can be said of you, the creator wants you to discover yourself and live your life to the fullest.

You cannot do all of the above without setting aside time to look deep into yourself. Meditation affords you this opportunity. Several people have a wrong view of meditation; some think it is an occult practice, while others believe that they need to spend a fortune to practice it. None of the above is entirely accurate. The kind of meditation I am talking about is that the one for which you deliberately set out time to do in a designated location, which keeps you from distractions, to enable you to think deeply about the questions that you need to answer in order to determine who you are truly.

This is what I want you to do: get away from all distractions, go and sit somewhere quiet, and start to imagine what you really want to do with your life; let your mind wander. I want you to think as big as possible, do not set any limitations on what you want. As you are indulging in a moment of introspection, start to ask yourself, 'What am I passionate about? What kind of gifts and talents do I possess? What has the creator put inside of me?' Keep imagining and asking yourself these questions until you find your answers. It can take you a day, weeks, or even months. It depends on how serious you are about discovering yourself. May I please add that when you do find the answer, I want you to stay true and pursue your inner self; not the life others want you to live, but the life you were created to live.

When you know who you truly are, and what you truly have, you will live happily, and be more productive.

DAY 5

TOPIC: **INTRODUCTION**

Do you feel like you are living without a purpose? Or perhaps you have a dream, but do not know how to achieve it? It could be that you have a vision for your life, you are also aware of what you need to do to realise this dream, but you have not really been able to organise yourself enough? What you need is **Goal Setting.**

After discovering yourself, setting goals is the next step towards preparing to live the kind of life you have always desired. Goal setting is critical to the development of skills and capacity in several areas of life. You need a comprehensive knowledge of the importance of goals, and the procedures used for goal setting, in order to achieve the greatness you desire.

Goals are the 'object or target of an action'. Goals are the competence level that you desire to attain or skills that you wish to acquire, which create a basis for assessing your current performance. Goals can be established over both the long and short term. While long-term goals can be regarded as the destination, short-term goals serve as directions that lead to that destination.

Goal setting is the process of choosing your destination, and creating a plan to reach it. You must have a target, and also design a plan that will help you achieve that aim. Goal setting helps you organise your actions. When you set goals, you know what to do within a specific time frame that will culminate in the achievement of your life vision.

To benefit from goal setting, it is essential that you not only decide what you want to do, but also create a plan to accomplish it. Several people find the latter difficult. They know what they want, and are enthusiastic about it, but they do not know how to create a plan that will take them to their desired destination.

In his book, *Think and Grow Rich*, Napoleon Hill tells the story of several ordinary individuals who rose to stardom using the principle of goal setting. My favourite is the story of a man named Bruce Lee. In 1971, this man became popular in China after performing a lead role in the film *Big Boss*, which later became one of his martial arts classics. Soon after achieving this feat, he moved to the United States and became the first renowned and fairly remunerated Asian actor in the country.

However, in 1969, Mr. Lee had documented his vision of becoming the highest-paid Oriental star in the United States. He referred to this as 'My Definite Chief Aim'. In Mr. Lee's words, what he desired was as follows:

'I, Bruce Lee, will be the first highest paid Oriental superstar in the United States. In return, I will give the most exciting performances and render the best of quality in the capacity of an actor. Starting 1970, I will achieve world fame, and from then onward till the end of 1980, I will have in my possession $10,000,000. I will live the way I please and achieve inner harmony and happiness'.

Even though Mr. Lee died in 1973, four years after documenting this goal, he accomplished it. My question to you is then have you written down your goals?

'The trouble with not having a goal is that you can spend your life running up and down the field and never score'. *Bill Copeland*

DAY 6

SUB-THEME: **GOAL SETTING**

TOPIC: **IMPORTANCE OF GOAL SETTING**

Yesterday, we discussed the meaning of goals and goal setting. However, I have heard people ask at different times, 'Are goals crucial? Can I not just become great without setting goals?' I can tell you, from my experience that goal setting remains one of the most critical steps you need to take in order to find your true calling and unparalleled success. Let us look, in detail, at the importance of goal setting.

Goals give you focus. If you do not have goals, your efforts will be disorganised. More often than not, you will be confused about what you ought to do at a particular time. Goals help you define and zero in on essential daily tasks, thereby preventing idle moments and wasted efforts.

Goals provide a gauge for measuring your progress. While pursuing success, many people get discouraged because after journeying for a long time, they feel like they have not reached their desired destination. At this point, several people give up and throw in the towel because they did not set adequate goals. Goals help you know that even though you are not yet at your destination, you have taken reasonable steps in the right direction. It is essential to measure your progress as you move towards greatness, but this is only achievable through goal setting.

Goals inspire and keep you motivated. It is easy to procrastinate when you do not have goals. For example, a footballer who does not have any goal can decide to skip working out on certain days when he does not feel like training. Conversely, one with a goal, say to become the highest scorer in the tournament, will do what he has to do whether he feels like it or not. He will go the extra mile even when he is tired. The goal will both motivate and keep him inspired.

According to the late motivational speaker Zig Ziglar, 'What you get by achieving your goals is not as important as what you become by achieving your goals'. When you set goals, you allow yourself to become a better person. First, you develop more confidence in your ability to get things done. The greatest thing that happened to me was becoming a better version of myself as I was going after my goals. I became more self-disciplined and consistent in my pursuit of building a strong character. As you go after your goals you will find that the person you are becoming is just as important, if not more, as the actual goals you are trying to accomplish.

Goal setting makes you aware of what it takes to reach your destination. Several people desire to achieve excellence in a particular field, but they do not know what they need to do to get there. A goal-setter would have done adequate research in the course of setting those targets and knows precisely what he needs to do. Whether he will do this or not is another topic, but a person who knows what to do at what time in order to achieve an aim is better than someone who doesn't.

> 'If you are bored with life—you do not get up every
> morning with a burning desire to do things—you
> do not have enough goals'.
>
> *Lou Holtz*

DAY 7

SUB-THEME: **GOAL SETTING**

TOPIC: **KEY PRINCIPLES OF GOAL SETTING**

To set goals that will fulfil the aims discussed the day before, there are guidelines to follow. If you do not follow these rules, you may not attain your goals. The principles for setting effective goals are discussed below.

Write down what you want. To make goal setting effective, you need to write down your goals. Previously, we read that Bruce Lee kept a written document about his goals and plans. My question to you is, 'Do you have a written document of your goals and plans?' The bible tells us in Habakkuk 2:2 to write down the vision and make it plain. When you write your life goals, you commit yourself to achieving them. I have a big black book in my house that I use to keep track of my goals. Inside my book, I list both long-term and short-term goals. Some of these goals are as short as my daily goals, while others are as longstanding as twenty years from now. One of the goals in my big black book is to write a book that will inspire people. This book is a testimony to the achievement of that goal.

A well-known maxim says, 'The faintest pen is sharper than the sharpest brain'. Do not assume that you will remember your goals, write them down. Penning your goals activates your mental powers, and helps your subconscious mind remain aware of these goals throughout the day. Write down your long- and short-term goals; break them into yearly, monthly, weekly, and daily targets. You do not yet need to know how to achieve them, or where the money will come from, just write down your goals. Furthermore, you must write your goals in the present tense. For instance, instead of writing, 'I will increase my wealth by 50%,' write, 'I am in the process of increasing my wealth by 50%'. Writing your goals in the present tense helps you stay motivated throughout the entire process.

Read your goals every morning and evening. This is one way to keep your mind focused on your goals. When your mind is conscious of your goals, you are motivated to achieve them. As I mentioned previously, I write down my goals in my big black book; this makes it easier to read them every morning when I wake up, and every evening before I go to bed. I read, meditate, and pray about my goals every day. The more often I read my goals, the more my mind gives me answers. In addition to reading your goals every morning and evening, ensure that you keep your mind conscious of your goals every moment of the day by writing your goals and pasting them in conspicuous locations where you can see them as you go through your daily activities. To make this more effective, divide your goals and place them in locations that relate to them. For instance, if you have a goal about losing weight, you can put that in your kitchen.

Find people who can help you achieve your goals. After I graduated from university, I was unemployed for three years. I was at a very low point in my life because I felt betrayed by the system. I did what was expected of me—I went to university and bagged a degree, but I could not land my desired high-paying job. Three years went by, and I kept receiving emails such as, 'Unfortunately you have been unsuccessful...' until one day I told myself that if no one was going to hire me, I would hire myself. I formed a goal to start an online TV media platform, but I was broke and had no equipment to get my company off the ground, so I started to brainstorm in my tiny bedroom. I thought about all the people that could help me with equipment, such as cameras, lights, and microphones, among others. I reached out to everyone who came to mind during my brainstorm, and in less than a month after calling every person on the list, I had my first company called UnashamedTV up and running. I went from being unemployed for 3 years to becoming the founder of an online TV media channel. This success was achieved by identifying the people that could help me with my goals. Take a look at your goals now, brainstorm, and ask yourself, 'Who or what can help me achieve my goals?'

We will continue with the others tomorrow.

'If you want to be happy, set a goal that commands your thoughts, liberates your energy, and inspires your hopes'.

Andrew Carnegie

DAY 8

SUB-THEME: **GOAL SETTING**

TOPIC: **PRINCIPLES OF GOAL SETTING 2**

Yesterday, we looked at some critical principles of goal setting. Today, we will consider some of the rules that you can apply.

Set a deadline for each goal. A goal without a deadline is just an idea. Your goals must have a time dimension attached to them; it is only by doing this that you can measure your progress effectively. For example, if you want to make $600 in 3 months, that means you must make at least $200 per month. It is easier to measure your progress at the end of each month. However, do not be too hard on yourself. If you do not reach your goal by your deadline, all you have to do is push the deadline back. I wanted to write my first book a few years back, but when I did not reach those targets, all I did was push back the timeline. Goals are there to add focus to your life, not pressure.

Set meaningful goals. You do not set goals for the fun of it; you set goals so that you can achieve them, and as a result, make your life better. Hence, your goals must resonate with your inner self.

It is useless to set wild goals that do not mean anything to you just to impress people, or to keep up with the Joneses. When you set meaningful goals, you'll be ready to do whatever it takes to realise them. The 'why' behind your goal is critical to its realisation. For example, if an individual set a goal to become wealthy because he wanted to have more bills with deceased prominent figures on them, I am sure you'll agree that it wouldn't take long before this person stopped pursuing the goal. When the pains of the hard work required to make money appear for the first time, such a person will not be able to withstand them. However, if you set a goal to become wealthy because you want financial freedom and security, you will be willing to work diligently to achieve that goal. You must always attach a reason to your goals, and ensure that the idea is meaningful to you.

Create an action plan. A lot of people miss this step when setting goals, but goal setting is useless if it does not affect your daily schedule. The secret of great men lies in their daily routine. Action plans are the things that you will do every day that will eventually culminate in the realisation of your goals. Your action plan should correspond to your goals. For example, if you want to lose 10 pounds of weight in 2 months, you need to work out for at least 30 minutes at least 4 times a week. Also, you will need to reduce fat intake. These are your action plans.

Now, you need to practice goal setting. Go through the fundamental principles again, set goals for a particular aspect of your life, and ensure that you apply the essential concepts described above.

'Success is the progressive realization of a worthy goal or ideal'.

Earl Nightingale

DAY 9

SUB-THEME: **TAKE ACTION**

TOPIC: **INTRODUCTION**

There is a famous maxim that says, 'The universe rewards action, not thoughts'. Action creates the divide between successful and unsuccessful individuals, winners and losers, high achievers, and ordinary people. Several people get caught up in the cage of scrutinising, scheduling, and organising to the point that they avoid taking action. It was John Ruskin who said, 'What we think or what we know or what we believe is, in the end, of little consequence. The only consequence is what we do'.

Have you ever seen someone take a giant stride towards achieving a goal, and you thought, 'That could have been me?' Have you been in a situation where another person implements a similar idea to the one you have? I bet there is no worse feeling than that. You have taken time to discover yourself, create goals and action plans, only to fail in the most critical part of the process, namely the execution.

I want you to solve this little arithmetic. There are 8 birds on a tree, but 4 of them decided to fly away. A hunter walks by and shoots at the tree. How many birds can the hunter kill? Did you say 4? You are incorrect. You see, as critical as making a decision is, it is very far from taking action. The fact that 4 birds decided to fly away does not mean that the bullets cannot still hit them. Yes, by choosing to fly, they have taken a first step in the right direction towards safety, but until they actually fly, they are still in danger. I want you to know that the distance between taking a decision and taking action is like the gap between heaven and earth. You can dream all you want, but until you take steps to achieve that goal, you remain a dreamer. You can set goals and plan effectively, but without actually following through on the plan, it remains a simple wish. A world-renowned maxim says, 'If wishes were horses, beggars would ride'.

Almost all the successful people in the world have one thing in common. Before becoming famous, they thought their ideas were not practicable. However, despite the rejections encountered, they chose to act on their dreams. They did not know that they would become as great as they are, but still decided to act all the same. Some of them were not even sure if their ideas would fail or succeed, yet they took action. Had they not acted, we would probably not have known them today. Taking action is the hallmark of highly successful people.

Matt Galligan, the CEO of Circa, opines that one of the most critical traits of any entrepreneur, is the ability to create balance between thinking through the process of solving a problem, and actually implementing the solution. On the one hand, there are people who do not take the time to observe issues and think about how they may be solved. On the other hand, there are others who spend too much time in the thinking stage to the point that they miss the opportunity to act, solve the problem, and become successful.

There is absolutely nothing that can replace taking action. Life only supports those who are proactive about their goals. An individual with a fantastic idea can die poor, while a person with a less practical idea can die wealthy and fulfilled. The difference lies in taking action. If you take the action required to implement a plan, you may succeed or fail. If you succeed, you will have significant benefits; if you fail, you would have learnt how not to do something. Either way, you will become a better person. However, if you do not take action, you will remain as you have always been.

'You do not have to be great to start, but you have to start to be great'.

Joe Sabah

DAY 10

SUB-THEME: **TAKE ACTION**

TOPIC: **BENEFITS OF TAKING ACTION**

Taking action is the one step that makes your dreams and goals work for you. It will benefit you little to spend all the resources you have on purchasing books, attending seminars, reading, and learning, if you do not take action based on what you have learnt. No matter who you are or what you know, your life only becomes meaningful when you take action.

Taking action is critical because it is the only way to get results. The action you choose determines the results you get. If you want to change something about your life, you need to take action. Several people wonder why their lives are not getting better. They are taking steps observing, planning, analysing, and criticising, so, they believe that their life is in motion. However, motion is different from action, and until you take action, you cannot get results. For instance, you will not lose a pound of weight just by reading about how to lose weight. You can attend all the health and fitness seminars you can find, but you won't lose an atom of weight until you begin to practice what you were taught. Goal setting only benefits you when you follow the action plan.

Taking action stops complaints. For example, if you complain that your house is not always tidy, it means that you are not doing things that will make your home neat. If you complain till you're blue in the face, nothing will change. But the day you take action, everything changes, and you stop complaining. You have peace of mind.

You can only overcome fear by taking action. Fear will keep you in a place known as your comfort zone. People who live in their comfort zones never amount to anything in life. You expand your comfort zone a bit every time you take action, and by doing so you prove to yourself that you can do the things that are necessary to bring the joy and peace you desire. Taking action puts you among the people who, despite fear, made great strides, and these are the only type of people that become successful.

You can only develop new skills and abilities when you take action. For instance, you do not learn to play football just by sitting in your room all day thinking about what you would do when the ball is passed to you. You have to step on the field and actually play the game for yourself. You will make mistakes, miss a few goals, but you will get better with time and practice. Also, taking action boosts your confidence. When you begin to take action, you stop engaging in negative self-talk, because you can see the results you are getting.

Life becomes more comfortable for others when you take action. For example, if you know how to solve a problem and you take the steps to implement the solution, you not only help yourself, but also society. When you help others, they will respect you more. Therefore, stop fighting for respect and recognition, and instead focus on taking action. Your results will bring you the recognition you desire.

Several people have regrets at old age because of the things they could have done when they were younger. I do not mean to spite you, but if you think about your past right now, you may also have regrets about a number of things that you should have done. However, no matter what the situation is, you can change things today if you start taking action. Just do what you are supposed to do, and your regrets in life will be minimal.

> 'Knowing is not enough; we must apply. Willing is not enough; we must do'.
>
> *Johann Wolfgang von Goethe*

DAY 11

SUB-THEME: **TAKE ACTION**

TOPIC: **COMMON HINDRANCES TO TAKING ACTION**

One of the most common obstacles to taking action is **FEAR.** Fear has been defined as 'False Expressions Appearing Real', or 'Forget Everything And Run'. Fear is a human emotion that sometimes keeps us from danger. For example, when you see a lion, you feel fear, and you run for safety. However, fear can also keep you from taking action on the crucial things that could move you forward.

There are different types of fear that prevent people from taking action. One such type is the fear of failure. You do not have to be afraid to fail, because success is cultivated from failure. I have not yet read the story of a single wealthy person who did not fail at one point or another. Walt Disney, for example, was relieved from working at The Kansas City Star paper in 1919. He did not commit any offence; the editor just felt that Disney was too dull and believed he could not generate creative enough ideas. Disney moved on from there and created his first animation company, which also failed. However, he continued and later created the Walt Disney Company, which went on to become a global success. He was nominated for the 59 Academy Awards.

Henry Ford, the founder of the Ford Motor Company, one of the most prosperous automotive firms of all time, also failed twice before founding the Ford Motor Company. In 1899, he started the Detroit Automobile Company. The company went bankrupt. Again, in 1901, he created the Henry Ford Company, but failed once more. The third attempt was the Ford Motor Company, which has blazed a new trail in the automobile industry.

You can read about any successful person in the world, whether dead or alive; all of them failed at some point. Therefore, you do not have to allow the fear of failure to keep you from taking the necessary action that could move you forward. Like Thomas Edison, who failed several times while trying to produce the electric light bulb, you must have the right perspective when it comes to failure. When asked how he coped with his perpetual failure, he responded, 'I have not failed. I've just found 10,000 ways that won't work'.

Another kind of fear that hinders people from taking action is the fear of taking a risk. There is a story about a sculptor who once had a guest in his studio. The guest was checking the artworks, and one of them caught his attention. The face of this statue was masked with hair, while the feet were covered with wings. 'The name of this sculpture is *Opportunity*,' said the sculptor. The guest was curious to know why the face of the sculpture was masked. 'Because people do not recognise opportunity when it comes,' replied the sculptor. The guest also asked why the feet of the sculpture were covered with wings. 'Because opportunity does not stay for long, it leaves quickly, and once it is gone, it can never be retrieved'. The mask covering opportunity is risk. If you do not want to take risks, you cannot move your life forward in a sufficiently impactful way.

Some people think that it is too risky for them to take action on their dreams and passions. But do you know what is truly risky? It is moving from one place to the other, living an unfulfilled life. Risky is doing what does not contribute to the realisation of your dreams. The worst person you can meet at the end of your life is the person you could have become, but didn't because of your fear of taking risks. If you must achieve your dreams, you need to rise now and take action despite your concerns!

> 'Stop standing in your own way. Stop making excuses. Stop talking about why you can't. Stop sabotaging yourself. Decide which direction you are going in and take action. One decision at a time, one moment at a time'.
>
> *Akiroq Brost*

DAY 12

TOPIC: COMMON HINDRANCES TO TAKING ACTION 2

Aside from the fear of failure and taking the risks that we discussed yesterday, there are other common obstacles to taking action. Some people wait until the conditions are perfect before they take action. What you need to know is that the circumstances for doing meaningful things will suck most times. If you look at the history of famous firms, you will discover that several of them were founded during economic depression. This is the case for Microsoft, LinkedIn, Standard Oil, among others. If you wait until the conditions are perfect, you will miss out on several opportunities to become great. Stop waiting for an ideal time, take the actions you can today. If you want to become the highest-paid broadcaster in the United States, you do not wait until you get a job with a broadcasting corporation before you start to take action. Even if all you have is your room, you can practise reading the news right there. The point I am making is that there is always something you can do regardless of where you are in your journey. Do not wait for your circumstances to be perfect. Start acting now!

Furthermore, some people refuse or stop taking action because they think they are not making progress. You need to know that your brain can mess with you because of the way it is wired. For example, if you want to lose 10 pounds of weight, and you start taking action in that direction, your brain can tell you that you are not making progress because you have not yet lost 10 pounds of weight. However, the truth is that you are still making progress. You need to know that progress does not always look or feel the way you might expect it to. But if you keep taking action in the right direction, you are surely making progress.

Also, several people refuse to take action because they think they need to know more. Knowledge is essential, but you need to start applying what you know while seeking to understand more. Some things can only be learnt while taking action. Have you ever seen anyone getting their driving licence just because of their theoretical knowledge of road signs and procedures? To be granted permission, you need actually to drive, you need to move the car. The authorities need to be sure that you can keep a straight line while driving. You cannot learn this just by going to class, you need to sit behind the wheels and drive. Seek knowledge, but apply what you already know.

Also, some people never take action because they are always talking about taking action. This seems like an oxymoron, but there's a wide gap between taking action and talking about taking action. Stop talking, start acting. Take this piece of advice by 17th century Spanish prose writer and philosopher, Baltasar Gracian, 'Be content to act, and leave the talking to others'.

> 'Knowledge is power: You hear it all the time, but knowledge is not power. It's only potential power. It only becomes power when we apply it and use it. Somebody who reads a book and does not apply it, they're at no advantage over someone who's illiterate. None of it works unless YOU work. We have to do our part. If knowing is half the battle, action is the second half of the battle'.
>
> *Jim Kwik*

DAY 13

SUB-THEME: **TAKE ACTION**

TOPIC: **TIPS FOR TAKING ACTION**

There are certain habits, practices, and general tips that can help you take action. Some of them are discussed below.

Have action plans. We discussed action plans briefly when we talked about goal setting. And I mentioned that goal setting is useless, unless it affects your daily schedule. Who you are is a derivative of what you do every day. So, if you decide to take action, you need to do so daily. Sometimes, taking action can seem daunting. For example, if you want to learn how to drive, you could be discouraged just by thinking about the number of things you have to learn, and the complexity of the driving process. But if you break everything down into bits, and do a bit every day, before long, you would have achieved your goal. For every dream you have, decide what you will do every day that will culminate in the realisation of that dream.

Overcome your fear. First, you need to be aware of your concern. In other words, you need to know precisely why you are afraid. When you find out why you are scared, also examine the veracity of that fear. For example, if you are afraid to take action because you failed before, think about how many other people there are who failed previously and later succeeded. And the fact that you failed in the past does not mean you will fail now. Now, face the fear and take action in spite of it. You use your activity to overcome your fear.

Focus on the present. Several people overthink the past to the point that they do not take action in the present. Also, many focus on the future so much that they forget the present. I want you to know that the present is what matters most. You can learn from the past, and you can plan for the future, but the lessons from the past and the plan for the future will all be useless if you do not take action in the present. A Chinese proverb says, 'The best time to plant a tree was 20 years ago, the second-best time is now'. If we planted the tree 20 years ago, we would have been enjoying the fruits today. However, if we do not plant the tree today, 20 years from now, we will still be where we are today, but with regrets. So, the best time to act is now. According to English novelist, George Eliot, 'It is never too late to be what you might have been'.

You need to eliminate distractions and commit yourself to taking action consistently. By doing this, you become used to taking action. Now, what is it that you wanted to do that you have not done? Can you list these things in your journal and start acting on them? Remember, if you want a change, you must take action.

'Let every man or woman here remember this, that if you wish to be great at all, you must begin where you are and with what you are. He who would be great anywhere must first be great in his own Philadelphia'.

Russel H. Conwell

DAY 14

SUB-THEME: **SACRIFICE**

TOPIC: **INTRODUCTION**

We live in a world where we see, read, and hear about successful people more easily than ever before. Search engines like Google, and social media platforms like Facebook, have given us more access to the happenings in the lives of others. Thus, several people desire success. However, only a small number appreciate the sacrifice that successful people had to make to become what they are today. The road to success is challenging, only sacrificial people can walk that path.

Lionel Messi and Cristiano Ronaldo are arguably the two greatest footballers that the world has ever known. Even though the duo differs in physical outlook and nationality, they seem to have discovered one of the greatest secrets to achieving greatness—sacrifice.

Both Messi and Ronaldo decided from the outset that they wanted not only to be good players, but the best. Therefore, they were ready and willing to do what it takes to get there. They did not only desire success, they paid the price to achieve the kind of success they wanted.

Both of them had to leave their countries to pursue their dreams. It was painful, but they were willing to do whatever it takes to achieve their desires. They are both ambitious, committed, and focused. It was Messi who said, 'You have to fight to reach your dream. You have to sacrifice and work hard for it'.

In 2012, at the Ballon d'Or gala, Messi said, 'I am used to being the last person to leave. I like being in the dressing room. I love football, and training sessions are part of football'.

Also, when he was playing for the Manchester United Football Club, Ronaldo would sneak into the gym for additional training after the regular training sessions, so that he could bring his body into the condition that would help him achieve his goals.

Sacrifice is the act of giving up something today, so that you can achieve your goals. Your dreams determine the sacrifice you need to make, while the sacrifices you make determine how much of your dream you will achieve. If you desire to live an extraordinary life, you must part with many of the things that characterise the ordinary one. If you want to live a life that is superior to everyone else's, you must be ready to give up what others are unwilling to sacrifice. If you desire to be the best footballer like Messi and Ronaldo, every day you must be willing to stay longer in the training room than they do. There is no magic here, if you want massive success, you have to sacrifice massively.

In economics, there is a concept called 'opportunity cost'. The primary proposition of this concept is that everything you do has a cost, which may be direct or indirect. For example, if you decide to read up some materials that will increase your chances of achieving your dreams, you have given up other activities that you could have engaged in at that time. Everything has a cost, nothing is essentially free. It is up to you to decide what you are willing to give up and what you are eager to retain. However, be sure that your decision will determine the level of success you achieve.

Life does not reward wishes, it rewards sacrifice. The single factor that determines whether your dream is attainable or not is your willingness to give what it takes to achieve your goal. If you sacrifice enough, you will realise your desires.

> 'He who would accomplish little must sacrifice little; he who would achieve much must sacrifice much; he who would attain highly must sacrifice greatly'.
>
> *James Allen*

DAY 15

SUB-THEME: **SACRIFICE**

TOPIC: **WHY SACRIFICE?**

As human beings, our desires, dreams, and goals differ. Your aspirations are different from mine. However, one fact that is common to everyone is that there is a price to pay for the realisation of the targets we have. It is impossible to achieve success without giving it what it demands. There is no shortcut, you must sacrifice. Some of the other reasons why sacrifice is necessary are discussed below.

In life, balance is an illusion; you cannot have it all. For example, you cannot be the world's best footballer and world's best 'sleeper' at the same time. You cannot hang out with friends all the time, partying, and having fun, and still be the best father. To achieve what you want, you will have to say 'no' to several other things.

To accomplish your desires, you need to be committed, dedicated, and focused. You have to put efforts into doing something significant about your dreams daily. However, you cannot achieve this without sacrifice. The world is full of distractions and you will have to give up these distractions to achieve what you want. The distractions do not have to be negative in themselves, but if they keep you from concentrating on this crucial dream, you will need to give them up.

Sacrifice builds your willpower and discipline. I am sure you agree with me that discipline is essential for a great life. If you eat all the food you have access to, you will never have a great body. If you sleep for as long as you desire, you will never become a great entrepreneur. Every successful person we know today has trained themselves to be highly disciplined. For example, Bill Gates stopped watching TV in his 20s, and he did not allow his daughters to use a cell phone until they were fully grown. If you are not disciplined, you cannot achieve a great life.

You need to sacrifice because most people are not willing to. If you desire to live an outstanding life, then this is some good news. Sacrifice separates you from the crowd. I want you to do something now—look out your window. First, look straight, then look up. What do you see? When you look straight, you are likely to see other buildings in the neighbourhood, cars, trees, among other things. When you look up, you see a space, with a few birds flying. In life, most people live on the ground, they only do the things that every other person does, and so, they are not exceptional. It is sacrifice that takes you from the ground, where too many people are competing, to the height of success where there are only very few people.

The consequence of not sacrificing enough is grave—a life full of regrets due to unfulfilled dreams, goals, and aspirations. I am sure that you do not want to look back 20 years from now and shed tears because you wasted golden opportunities that could have made you great because you refused to give up temporary pleasure. What you lose by sacrificing is nothing compared to what you lose by being complacent. Do not think about the present alone, think about the future as well.

Until you begin to make the necessary sacrifices, your life will stay the same. Everything has a price—the success you desire, the heights you want to reach, the goals you want to accomplish all have a cost. If you do not pay your dues, you will pay the price of missing out on what you really want in life. The choice is yours. However, I encourage you to choose to sacrifice for the realisation of your dreams and begin NOW!

'Great achievement is usually born of great sacrifice and is never the result of selfishness'.

Napoleon Hill

DAY 16

SUB-THEME: **SACRIFICE**

TOPIC: **THINGS TO SACRIFICE**

Even though what you need to give up in order to achieve your dream is 'whatever it takes,' discussed below are some of the common things that successful people give up to achieve greatness.

Sacrifice who you are. One of the most significant sacrifices you will need to make to achieve what you desire is to change who you are for who your dreams need you to become. You can read that again. Your goals will require that you alter the way you think, the habits you indulge, and the beliefs you hold on to, among others. For example, if you want to become a great entrepreneur, but you are naturally shy, you will need to sacrifice that timidity and learn to be bold. If you must become a great leader, you need to adopt behaviours that help excellent leaders succeed. You have to be willing to give up who you are at this present moment for who you need to become to realise your dreams. If you remain in your comfort zone, you will never accomplish your targets.

Sacrifice time. Time is a leveller. In other words, every human being has the same amount of this resource—we all have 24 hours in a day. To achieve your desires, you must sacrifice time. What do I mean by sacrifice time? An average person likes to sleep for about 8 hours every day, but I am yet to read about any great person who sleeps for 8 hours daily. Even the Bible says in Proverbs 6:10-11 that chronic poverty awaits those who sleep too much. You must get off your bed as early as possible and work on your goals. If you are working a job and you have your dreams, you need to sleep less. I am not saying that you shouldn't rest at all, I am talking about excessive sleep. You need to sacrifice excessive sleep to achieve success. Also, you sacrifice time by apportioning quality time to the activities that bring you closer to the realisation of your targets on a day to day basis. For example, if you want to become a great athlete, you need to dedicate quality time to working out and practice daily. However, if you want to become the best entrepreneur, you need to give quality time to reading about businesses daily. You cannot achieve your dreams if you spend all your time playing video games, unless your dream is to become the best video game player. The point is to minimise to the barest minimum the number of activities that do not relate to your goals, so that you can focus on the ones that bring you closer to achieving your dreams.

Sacrifice conflicts. Some people make other necessary sacrifices for the achievement of their dreams in addition to avoiding conflicts. The truth is that you need your mind to achieve your goals. If you allow conflicts to take over your mind, you will become less productive in the pursuit of your targets. The fewer conflicts you have in your life, the higher the propensity to accomplish your desires. One essential conflict that you must sacrifice to achieve your dream relates to incompatible goals. You cannot be a Mark Zuckerberg and a Lionel Messi at the same time. You cannot be a Bill Gates and a Cristiano Ronaldo at the same time. You have to sacrifice one of the goals, or you wouldn't achieve any.

Furthermore, you must resolve incompatible responsibilities. You must develop the courage to say 'no' to several propositions to commit to things that do not align with your dream. If you can cut off these conflicts, you will realise that you have more time, energy, and resources to focus on your goal.

> 'You can't sleep. Broke people sleep. You got to be willing to sacrifice sleep; if you sleep, you may miss the opportunity to be successful'.
>
> *Eric Thomas*

DAY 17

SUB-THEME: **SACRIFICE**

TOPIC: **THINGS TO SACRIFICE 2**

Yesterday, we discussed some things that successful people sacrifice to achieve greatness. Let us conclude on them today.

Sacrifice instant gratification. To achieve the kind of life you desire, you may need to give up the safe, secure, and comfortable life you are living at the moment. For example, Mark Zuckerberg, the founder of Facebook and the 5th richest man in the world, was faced with a decision of whether to continue studying at Harvard University or drop out to focus on Facebook. He chose to drop out. In his words, 'It took me five minutes to decide that I was going to drop out'. By doing this, he sacrificed the instant gratification of being a Harvard student for his dreams. Also, at a point, Yahoo offered to purchase Facebook for $100,000,000. He declined the offer because he believed in his dreams. Several of his management team members thought that selling Facebook was the best thing to do at that time, but Mark was adamant to delay gratification. Today, Facebook is the most popular social media platform in the world, and it has been the primary source of Mark's wealth. To achieve the kind of life you desire, you need to channel your resources towards activities that relate to your dream. My friend told me that one time he went to see one of his friends perform at an art gallery. There was a young guy who also played at the gallery that day. His performance was unique and intriguing. One of his lyrics went thus, 'There is hunger in my belly'. The crowd was enjoying the lyrics and singing along with him. The performance was awe-inspiring. When he concluded his performance, my friend approached him and praised him. The artist replied that the reason the crowd was feeling him was because he was living his lyrics. He said he had not eaten in the past 24 hours because he had limited financial resources. He had to choose between using the money to buy food or using it to get a train ticket to perform at the art gallery. He decided to purchase the train ticket because he knew that there could be rich people inside the art gallery, who would invest in his dreams, and once they have invested, he could buy any kind of food he liked. He chose to delay gratification, and give the performance instead. He sacrificed his meal because he knew that his dream was way bigger than that one meal. To achieve your goals, you need to give up the idea of seeking instant gratification.

The things people sacrifice to achieve their dreams are endless; however, you must know that what you need to sacrifice is whatever it takes. I only mentioned these things as a guide. You must think about your goals critically, determine what it will take to achieve those goals, and go all out to 'give it whatever it takes'. Do not settle for your comfort zone, step out and make the necessary sacrifices for your dreams. Do not forget that it is your dreams that determine the kind of sacrifices you need to make, and the level of sacrifice you are willing to make determines how much of your dream you will achieve.

> 'The most important decision about your goals is not what you are willing to do to achieve them, but what you are willing to give up'.
>
> *Dave Ramsey*

DAY 18

SUB-THEME: **SACRIFICE**

TOPIC: **THINGS TO NEVER SACRIFICE**

The purpose of seeking to achieve greatness is to live a happy and fulfilled life, and making sacrifices is a vital tool to realise that desire. However, several people have made significant mistakes in their pursuit of greatness, in that they sacrificed the things they should have held dear. When these people achieve their goals, they still live with regrets and sorrow. Some of the things you should never sacrifice are discussed below.

Your family. While it is true that you need to dedicate time to the pursuit of your goals, ensure that you do not leave your family out, because after you have achieved all the wealth you desire, you will come to realise that it is the connection to your family that will give you the happiness and sense of fulfilment that you want. What is the benefit of being an accomplished entrepreneur when your children are wayward because they lacked care? As you set ambitious goals for yourself, make sure that you dedicate just as much to your family. Be careful to make enough time for your spouse and children.

Your health. There is an adage that says, 'Health is wealth; when wealth is lost, nothing is lost; but when health is lost, all is lost'. While I will not tell you to sleep for ten hours every day, it is still important that you get sufficient rest—make this part of your goal. It is only a person who is alive that can pursue the realisation of other dreams, therefore, your top priority should be to remain healthy. The exciting fact about keeping healthy is that it does not require a lot. All you need to do is to rest well, eat well, and exercise well. If you think you are so busy that you cannot sleep well, very soon, you will be forced to rest, most times in a hospital. If you think you do not have enough resources to eat well now, you will soon find out that the cost of purchasing medication is way higher than the price of eating a balanced diet every day. If you wait till things get out of hand, you will spend more money and time on treatment. I am not saying that you cannot sacrifice sleep, food, and exercise once in a while, but it should not be your way of life, because soon enough, you will realise that you cannot cheat nature.

Other things that you should not sacrifice include integrity, honesty, your identity, and your relationships, among others. Ensure that before making any sacrifice for your dreams, you take into account the cost, whether the sacrifice is worth it in the end or not.

'Man surprised me most about humanity. Because
he sacrifices his health in order to make money.
Then, he sacrifices money to recuperate his health.

And then he is so anxious about the future that he does not enjoy the present; the result being that he does not live in the present or the future; he lives as if he is never going to die, and then dies having never really lived'.

Dalai Lama

DAY 19

....

SUB-THEME: ENDURANCE

....

TOPIC: INTRODUCTION

Sometimes, when people are exposed to motivational words, like the ones you have been reading in this devotional from day one, they decide to make significant changes to their lives. Some set goals, while others go a step further to act in ways that are consistent with their plans. A lot of people get astonishing results within the first few weeks of attempting to follow their dreams, but the usual regrettable experience is that many people slide back into what they used to be after a couple of months.

Sociologist Josh Morgan studied the number and state of podcasts on iTunes from 2005 to 2015. The findings of the study revealed that the average podcast lasted only about 6 months, and had 12 episodes (2 episodes per month). Also, most of the podcasts did not garner as much as a single rating. The most alarming part of the findings is that only about 40% of the podcasts were active at the time of the study. This means that about 60% of podcasters have quit.

Angela Duckworth revealed an interaction between a young man and herself in her book, *Grit: The Power of Passion and Perseverance*. This young man, a college student, wanted to start a podcast to inspire, motivate, and enlighten entrepreneurs. Duckworth questioned him about what he would do if he became weary of the project. The young man replied that he would start another podcast. This young man thought that the best thing was to start something else when you are fed up with what you are currently doing.

Well, the stories above talk about others. Can you please take a moment to reflect? How many projects have you started that you abandoned? Those things you were enthusiastic about three years ago, did you pursue them to mastery? I am not about to judge or condemn you, but I am planning to show you why people start something they really want to do but stop at some point along the way. I am about to expose the 'demon' that prevents people from seeing essential things through to completion. That 'demon' is called a lack of endurance.

Endurance is the capacity to withstand the tendency to quit after doing something challenging for a long time. It is a crucial quality for individuals who desire to achieve greatness in life. To endure is to keep moving despite difficulties, stress, hardship, or trials. Endurance is the resolution never to give up, the determination to press on, and the resilience to remain focused. It is closely associated with patience.

According to Caroline Myss, a five-time New York Times bestselling author and globally celebrated speaker in the fields of science, medical intuition, human consciousness, health, and energy medicine, 'Without the capacity to endure, you are impatient, demanding, short-tempered, and you tend to abandon projects that you are meant to complete because you cannot immediately see their significance... With endurance, you know that you can survive anything that is asked of you'.

You grow your capacity to endure every time you resist the temptation to quit doing something beneficial to your life. Most people do not have a problem with being enthusiastic, the only challenge is enduring. I am optimistic that by the time you are done reading this part about endurance, you will have developed a die-hard resolve to achieve your goals and dreams no matter what comes your way.

> 'All you can do is all you can do, but all you can do
> is enough. The secret is sustaining the effort to do
> "all you can do"'.
>
> *A. L. Williams (founder of Primerica)*

DAY 20

TOPIC: THE RELATIONSHIP BETWEEN ENDURANCE AND SUCCESS

Thomas Edison, one of the world's greatest scientists, said that the first prerequisite for success is 'the ability to apply your physical and mental energies to one problem without growing weary'. He also demonstrated this by staying put after failing multiple times in his quest to invent the light bulb. It is said that he failed 10,000 times in this process. The level of success you can attain is directly proportional to the amount of pain you are willing and able to endure.

Have you noticed that all of the wealthiest people in the world have something for which they are known? Warren Buffet is known for investments; Bill Gates is known for Microsoft; Jeff Bezos is known for Amazon; Mark Zuckerberg is known for Facebook, and so on. What was the one significant factor that binds all these people together? Endurance. Imagine if they had quit at every challenge; they would not have been as successful as they are today.

One of the greatest virtues of successful people in any field is endurance. The road to success and greatness is laced with pain, and your capacity to endure this pain and move on determines how much success and greatness you can achieve. People do not become great effortlessly, every great person has learnt to endure.

Greatness is persevering for one more moment. If you can stand firm when others are sitting, you will achieve the level of success that others cannot reach. Endurance involves converting life's challenges to conduits of progress and prosperity. Everyone who ever accomplished anything worthwhile had something to endure. I wish I could say that again. Do not be deceived, it takes more than mere passion and initial enthusiasm to achieve excellence. You must be willing and able to endure pain.

The truth of life is that strength, character, and the realisation of your goals are achieved through pain. For instance, human body experts have said that it is through pain that the muscles are built. That is, if you desire to develop your muscles and you hit the gym, it is when you start feeling the pain that your muscles start forming. If you stop, you will not achieve our desire, but if you carry on despite the pain, you will soon see the results. Also, if you desire to change a bad habit, you cannot achieve that without enduring some pain. It was Helen Keller, an American author, political activist, lecturer and the first deaf-blind person to earn a Bachelor of Arts degree, who said, 'Character cannot be developed in ease and quiet. Only through experience of trial and suffering can the soul be strengthened, ambition inspired, and success achieved'.

You can accomplish whatever you set your mind to in life, as long as you are prepared to endure the difficulties, pains, and setbacks that are part of the journey to success, greatness, and happiness without losing your enthusiasm and optimism. History is replete with stories of people who endured pain without losing faith. You can be one of them!

> 'Many of life's failures are people who did not realize how close they were to success when they gave up'.
>
> *Thomas Edison*

DAY 21

SUB-THEME: **ENDURANCE**

TOPIC: **MINDSETS THAT EMPOWER YOU TO ENDURE**

According to Mahatma Gandhi, an Indian lawyer, and political ethicist, who led the successful campaign for India's independence using nonviolent resistance, 'Your beliefs become your thoughts, your thoughts become your words, your words become your actions, your actions become your habits, your habits become your values, your values become your destiny'. Essentially, what this means is that the foundational building block of everything you do and become is your mindset or your belief system. It is safe to say that your mindset will determine whether you will endure pain or not. Today, we will look at some of the mindsets that help you endure hardship on your way to greatness.

Failure is an opportunity to learn. If you have the mindset that failure gives you the privilege of learning, you will be willing to endure the scourge of failure as you seek to achieve greatness. In an interview, Thomas Edison was asked how he managed to continue the research that led to the invention of the light bulb despite multiple failed attempts. He replied by saying that he did not fail, he only learnt a number of ways that did not work. When you try something, and it does not work out as expected, do not consider yourself a failure. Instead, see this as learning how not to do what you are looking to accomplish.

Challenges make you grow. Several people think that their problems are there to pull them down; as such, they cannot endure. However, if you develop the mindset that challenges are opportunities for you to better yourself, you will build your capacity to endure hardship. I believe it is essential to find out if problems truly make people grow. Let us take the school system, for example. Every time students are to move to the next class, they are required to write exams. If a student thinks that the school teacher hates him, he may choose not to prepare for the exam because of the pain of studying diligently. However, a student who believes that the teacher wants him to write the exam so he can move to the next class will endure the pain of studying. The results will most likely be that the former will fail and have to repeat the course, while the latter will succeed and move to the next class, thereby, increasing his knowledge, social status, and value. When you overcome a challenge, you do not remain at the same level you were before you encountered the difficulty, you move higher, you learn something new.

My attitude, not my feelings determine my future. Some people live based on how they feel, but they fail to realise that emotions and feelings are transient. Your feelings do not determine your future. Therefore, it would be unwise to quit something that you know will be profitable to your life because of how you feel. You have to develop the mindset that whether you feel like it or not, you must do what you need to do to accomplish the future that you desire. For example, it does no longer matter how Thomas Edison felt after each failed attempt, what matters today is that he had the right attitude. It is human to feel bad when something does not go as planned, but that feeling in itself does not determine whether you can still achieve success or not; it is your attitude that is the ultimate determinant of the level of greatness that you can achieve.

I only raised these points as an introduction to some of the mindsets that can empower you to endure. You need to take some time out to think about the mindsets that encouraged the abandonment of projects that you initiated in the past. Write them down, and begin to develop new mindsets that will empower you to endure pain, hardships, and difficulties as you seek to achieve greatness.

> 'Nothing in the world can take the place of perseverance. Talent will not; nothing is more common than unsuccessful people with talent. Genius will not; unrewarded genius is almost legendary. Education will not; the world is full of educated derelicts. Perseverance and determination alone are omnipotent'.
>
> *Calvin Coolidge*

DAY 22

TOPIC: **HOW TO DEVELOP YOUR CAPACITY FOR ENDURANCE**

Discussed below are some of the ways that you can use to develop your resilience.

Stop Dabbling. A lot of people subscribe to the jack-of-all-trades mentality. Once they encounter little difficulty while making efforts to achieve a goal or learn a skill, they drop it and move to another one. These kinds of people do not become professionals or master of anything, they just dabble around. It was Tony Robbins, an American author, life coach, and public speaker listed on the Worth Magazine Power 100 list in 2015 and 2016, who said, 'If you want lasting change, you have got to give up this idea of "trying something." You have got to decide you are going to commit to mastery. Most people dabble. They say, "I would like to change my body" or "I would like to make my relationship better." These people do not have enough details to follow through'. It is easy to dabble than to stay put with a dream. Dabblers never admit that they gave their all to something and it failed. You must know that dabbling is not one of the formulas for achieving greatness. Steve Jobs, an American business magnate and co-founder of Apple Inc., said, 'I am convinced that about half of what separates the successful entrepreneurs from the non-successful ones is pure perseverance'. You need to decide to stop dabbling, select a course of action, and stay put until you achieve the success and greatness you desire.

Celebrate your successes. Some people cannot endure because they have a flawed view of success. They think success means attaining the ultimate goal and do not realise that success is the progressive movement in the right direction towards their goals. For example, if your goal is to become the best surgeon in the world, you succeed when you complete each of the exams that take you to the next level in school. You thrive when you begin to practice general medicine. You thrive when you take your specialisation exams and pass them. You succeed when you handle a surgical case well. You should celebrate all these little successes, even though you are yet to reach your ultimate goal. Taking note of these successes will help you endure until you achieve your dream. When we discussed goal setting, I mentioned that you must have action plans—things you will do daily that will culminate in the achievement of your dreams. If you can focus on achieving success following your action plans, you will surely develop the capacity to endure. In other words, you live one day at a time.

Connect with others. Sometimes, you need others who desire greatness as much as you do to stay on track. Look out for people with a similar mindset, and build a connection with them. They will encourage you when you are down, and you will inspire them as well. You must indeed be wary of keeping too many friends; however, that does not mean you should be a lone ranger. I believe that there is at least one person around you that is passionate about greatness like you; discover and connect with them. Thanks to social media, these days, you can connect with people that are not even within your geographical location, who will motivate and inspire you to persevere. You can connect with me as well, listen to my videos, and get inspired.

> 'Most of the important things in the world have been accomplished by people who have kept on trying when there seemed to be no hope at all'.
>
> *Dale Carnegie*

DAY 23

SUB-THEME: **AVOID EXCUSES**

TOPIC: **INTRODUCTION**

In 1978, a candidate with two university degrees and a few postgraduate accomplishments ran for congress. He laboured diligently by doing all that was required, yet he lost the election by six percentage points. Also, in 2000, another candidate ran for congress but lost the election by a margin of 2 to 1. However, on the 20th day of January 2008, the former had a handshake with the latter as he passed him the presidency of the United States of America. I am referring to no other men than George Bush and Barack Obama, the 43rd and 44th presidents of the United States of America.

Are you wondering why I told you about these men? I wanted to explain to you that there are two kinds of people in the world—those that find an excuse, and those that get results. These two men belong to the category of those that get results. I hope you can imagine what it means to lose an election to the congress by such a small margin, the emotional trauma, the loss of resources, among others. Both men could have refused to try again, holding on to the excuse that they failed once, but they would have missed out on the possibility of living in the White House. Never forget this, 'Unsuccessful people find reasons for not achieving results, while successful people get results despite unfavourable reasons'.

Excuses are mental assertions that provide false relief for anyone who has decided (unintentionally) not to succeed. Several people use excuses to justify their lack of decisiveness when it comes to the pursuit of their goal. Usually, one would feel bad for not pursuing their dreams, but people use excuses to free themselves from the guilt of abandoning their life purposes. People who make excuses always have a reason to justify not doing what they ought to do.

Again, I want you to take some time to reflect. Just think about the way you lived in the past. Can you remember some of the excuses you came up with for not pursuing your dreams? How many times did you conclude that you cannot get something done even before trying it out? How many opportunities to connect with people have you missed out on because you thought they would not like you? How many times have you said 'I can't' about something that should have made you a better person?

Now, imagine if Steve Jobs and his partner, Steve Wozniak, had waited till they had enough money to rent an office space before starting their business. Imagine if they did not take advantage of what they had at that moment, and not started from where they were. We would probably not have Apple Inc. today. There will always be one reason or the other not to do what you are supposed to do to move your life forward. Every successful person had a choice between excuses and results, but they all chose results, and that is why we can read about their lives today.

The point here is not to make you cry because of the past; the aim is to stir your heart to the realisation of the importance of learning to overcome the propensity to make excuses. In the next few days, we will discuss excuses in more detail. I want you to prepare your mind. The past is gone, but you can decide that from today, you will no longer focus on reasons, only results.

> 'Ninety-nine per cent of the failures come from people who have the habit of making excuses'.
>
> *George Washington Carver*

DAY 24

TOPIC: **SALIENT FACTS ABOUT EXCUSES**

You need to be aware of some essential truths about excuses. The first is that there is always a good reason to make an excuse. For example, if you grew up in a rough neighbourhood, your parents might warn you never to interact with strangers. Also, if one of your relatives has lost money in business, you might believe that business is too risky. However, these well-meaning reasons can become stumbling blocks later in life. For instance, you do indeed need to be wary of strangers, but what if that stranger is the person you need to take the next leap towards success? What if that stranger is a potential life or business partner? Also, instead of assuming that business is risky because someone you know failed at it, why not find out the reason for their failure? At least several other people have succeeded in business. You need to examine all the logical reasons you have for not pursuing your goals before accepting them. Do not refuse to try something that you believe is meaningful to you because someone else failed at it.

Another fact that you need to know about excuses is that the more you make them, the more comfortable you become making more. Similarly, you become better at implementing an action that you take repeatedly. This is the way people become overweight. They begin with eating an extra dessert, missing one gym session, and watching one new movie. Before long, eating right and exercising frequently becomes an idea that lived in the past. The point here is that when you do something repeatedly, you become better at it, whether good or bad. Excuses are no different. However, according to Benjamin Franklin, one of the founding fathers of the United States, and world-renowned scientist and inventor, 'He that is good for making excuses is seldom good for anything else'. Therefore, if you start making excuses, it won't be long before you discover that you can rarely get anything meaningful done anymore. The reverse is also true. When you avoid making one excuse, you become more comfortable dissuading yourself from creating the next one. Soon enough, your life would have significantly moved forward because you would have focused on results, rather than excuses.

What I want you to know is that you cannot be good at making excuses and getting results at the same time, you will have to pick one. You cannot make excuses and make money at the same time; you cannot make excuses and raise an excellent family at the same time; you can either wait for something to happen, or you can make things happen. You cannot have it all. The relationship between making excuses and getting results is inversely proportional. That is, the more you commit to making excuses, the fewer results you get, and the more you commit to getting results, the fewer excuses you make.

Another fact I want you to understand is that excuses do not make your life better. You will indeed feel good temporarily, but in the long run, you would have become less excellent than you ought to be. Excuses will make you blind to opportunities that could lead to greatness. When you make excuses on a regular basis, you will lose credibility, and this can result in loss of job, family, and even life.

> 'Your complaints, your drama, your victim mentality, your whining, your blaming, and all of your excuses have NEVER gotten you even a single step closer to your goals or dreams. Let go of your nonsense. Let go of the delusion that you DESERVE better and go EARN it! Today is a new day!'
>
> *Steve Maraboli*

DAY 25

SUB-THEME: **AVOID EXCUSES**

TOPIC: **COMMON REASONS WHY PEOPLE MAKE EXCUSES**

The reasons behind excuses are indeed unique to individuals and their circumstances. Yet, I have discovered through observation and study that there are common factors that perpetuate the tendency to make excuses. I believe that an appropriate awareness of these underlying factors will better prepare you to overcome them. Let us start by having a look at the list below.

Fear. I can say that this is the most basic motivation for making excuses. When you are afraid, you amplify all the reasons why you should not do what you are supposed to do. There are different kinds of fear that propel people to make excuses—the fear of failure, the fear of making mistakes, the fear of the unknown, or the fear of uncertainty, just to name a few. This feeling of dread will inspire you to convince yourself that you need to remain in your comfort zone. I want you to know that fear is often the result of ignorance. Therefore, if you are afraid of getting something done, find out why you are so scared. Also, seek education to counter your fears. Solomon, the wisest king that ever lived, said in Ecclesiastes 1:9 that there is nothing new under the sun. Invariably, this means that there is no challenge you are currently facing that someone else has not gone through before. Seek out those people and find out how they scaled through. By doing so, your fears will diminish. Also, you must know that failure and mistakes are inevitable in life. They are part of the journey to greatness. Do not allow fear to make you cringe, do not relapse into your comfort zone by making excuses.

Lack of a specific goal. We have discussed goal setting in detail earlier in this book. If you are yet to create your goals, I advise you to go back and read the entire sub-theme on goal setting and develop specific goals for every area of your life. Without specific goals, excuses are inevitable. For example, if you decide that you will be wealthy, you can afford to make an excuse for not meeting a deadline by convincing yourself that it will not affect your overall wealth. However, if you have a goal to make $1000 in 2 months, you will be more diligent because you know that every dollar counts. When your destination is not clear, you can avoid a path because it is narrow. However, when you have a defined goal, and you know the path to that destination is a narrow road, you are more likely to do everything it takes to walk through that narrow road.

Unhealthy comparison. When you begin to compare yourself with others, you are setting yourself up for a life of excuses. When I started my online TV platform in 2015, I did not have a professional camera. If I compared myself with others, I would have had a reason to, but instead I focused on getting results. I used what I had, I started where I was. If you keep comparing yourself to others, you will not do things that will move your life forward; quit the comparison. Decide what you want and start with what you have.

Unwillingness to make a change. Several people are stuck in their way of life to the point that they do not desire to make any change at all. There is a difference between someone that cannot change and an individual that does not want to change. A person that thinks he cannot change can be helped by education, but a person that does not want to change will remain as he is. If you decide to keep doing things the way you have been doing them so far, you will keep making excuses. I challenge you to take a bold step today to eliminate excuses from your life.

> 'I had to make my own living and my own opportunity. But I made it! Do not sit down and wait for the opportunities to come. Get up and make them'.
>
> *Madam C. J. Walker*

DAY 26

SUB-THEME: AVOID EXCUSES

TOPIC: HOW TO STOP MAKING EXCUSES

The first point I want to make today is that no one can help you stop making excuses, you can only help yourself. Even though other people can make excuses for you, only you can eliminate excuses from your life. Yes, I will provide guidelines that could help you, but if you do not want to be helped, any effort will be futile. Therefore, I want you to stop reading for a while and think deeply before reading the principles that will help you eliminate excuses from your life. Why do you want to eliminate excuses from your life? What are the dreams, goals, and aspirations that excuses have cost you? Are the reasons you've identified strong enough to motivate you to elevate your life? If your answer to the last question is 'NO', you can close this book, and come back to it when you have discovered a strong enough purpose that makes it worth it to eliminate excuses from your life.

Now that you have discovered the 'why' behind your decision to eliminate excuses from your life, you have passed the first and most crucial stage. Let us look at a few guidelines that could help you move further.

Take responsibility. Never blame another person for your predicaments, always find a way to take responsibility for everything that happens to you. Being responsible means using all the resources available to you to solve the problems that you encounter. The first part of being responsible is accepting the consequences of your actions, while the other part is taking action to help others. If you have not pursued your goal in a while, rather than saying you were too busy, admit that you did not manage your time effectively. You must know that you can neither determine what others will do to you nor regulate the challenges that you will experience, but you can certainly control the way you respond to them.

Act daily. Like I mentioned a couple of days ago, you get better at whatever you do consistently. If you take regular action, in time, you will get better at it. I also mentioned that the relationship between making excuses and taking actions that yield results is inversely proportional. That is, an increase in one causes a decrease in the other. Therefore, if you take small steps daily towards the fulfilment of your goals, you will make fewer excuses. Develop an action plan for your goals—something you will do every day that will culminate in the achievement of your desires —and follow it strictly.

You have to be optimistic about life and focus on your strengths, not your weaknesses. Seek education and be well informed about your goals. Make friends with people who prioritise results. Take one step at a time and start with simple decisions. Soon enough, you will discover that you have successfully eliminated excuses from your life.

'Stop making excuses and start producing results'.
Rudolf O. Brenyah

DAY 27

....

SUB-THEME: OVERCOME PROCRASTINATION

....

TOPIC: INTRODUCTION

In the world we live in, several factors contribute to our failure to achieve our goals. Some of them include lack of resources, personnel, or connections to name a few. However, the most significant element that makes people unable to achieve their dreams is **PROCRASTINATION**. People who procrastinate are their own problems, they are responsible for their own undoing.

Procrastination is the habit of deferring something that should be done now to a later time. It is doing low-priority work in place of high-priority work. It is not the same as scheduling or prioritising. When you schedule, you have a plan that dictates when and how you get work done. However, when you procrastinate, you put off tasks that seem to be challenging and concentrate on more leisurely activities. For example, if you planned to visit another country, but due to civil war in that country, you postponed the visit, you have not procrastinated. However, if you are to write a book, but you end up wasting time watching a movie, that is procrastination.

Procrastination has left many people with regrets at their death beds. One of them is the famous Leonardo da Vinci, who was well known as the ultimate genius of the Italian Renaissance. No doubt, Leonardo was extremely talented and contributed significantly to fields such as architecture, engineering, physics, botany, among others. He also explored sculpture-making, painting murals and portraits, and designed some machines that were not in use at the time he lived, such as submarines, helicopters and aeroplanes. However, Leonardo never met deadlines and always finished projects later than scheduled. Most of his efforts ended in unfinished projects. For example, he did not complete his works titled 'The Adoration of the Magi,' and 'Jerome in the Wilderness'. With some of the works that he had completed, he spent a lot of time on them. For example, it took 16 years to complete the 'Mona Lisa', which is his most famous work to date. Also, he completed London's National Gallery version of 'The Virgin of the Rocks' in just 13 years. Sometimes, clients had to threaten him before he could complete a project. For example, one time, his patron, Ludovico Sforza, the Duke of Milan, told Leonardo that he would cut off funds if he didn't complete the task he was assigned on time. It was only after this threat that Leonardo completed 'The Last Supper'. Towards the end of his life, Leonardo regretted the habit of procrastination. He felt the pain of not completing any project in the expected time and prayed to God to tell him if he did anything. After Leonardo died in 1519, several sketches of his unfinished projects were found in his codices.

Procrastination gives you a temporary sense of ease, because you are doing an easy or pleasurable task. It makes you feel you are productive, but in reality, you are not. It was Abraham Lincoln, one of the greatest Presidents that America ever had who said, 'You cannot escape the responsibility of tomorrow by evading it today'. When you procrastinate, you do not reach your full potential. If you can achieve 100 things, procrastination will make you accomplish less than 10. It is a habit that you must address before you can achieve greatness.

In the next few days, we will explore procrastination in more detail. I want you to prepare your mind. Take some time out to think about the things you have lost because you procrastinated, the reasons why you procrastinate, and how you have coped in the past. I will share some insights with you, but I want you to meditate on these points first. It will help you apply what you will read effectively.

'My advice is, never do tomorrow what you can do today. Procrastination is the thief of time. Collar him!'

Charles Dickens

DAY 28

SUB-THEME: OVERCOME PROCRASTINATION

TOPIC: THE DOWNSIDES OF PROCRASTINATING

Procrastination can have several adverse effects not only on your productivity, but life in general. For example, imagine a fire broke out, and you call the fire brigade, but the person on duty decides to procrastinate answering the call. That act could result in the death of several hundreds of people. Sometimes, the difference between life and death is a moment of action. If you defer that action, several people will lose their lives. I bet you do not want to live with the guilt of having people lose their lives because you deferred something you could have done.

Aside from the loss of life, procrastination wastes your time. Some people act as if they will live forever, but the truth is that time waits for no one. You may dilly-dally, but time does not. While you are busy putting off productive work that you should get done, time is busy trickling away. You might wake up one day and discover that five years have passed, and nothing has changed. At that time, you will regret the time you wasted. The most painful part will be that you cannot pull back the hands of time, you cannot go back and do what you were supposed to do. You do not deserve this kind of regret at old age. You deserve to fulfil your dreams. As such, you should overcome procrastination.

Procrastination makes you miss life-changing opportunities. More often than not, opportunities come to people disguised as challenges. If you have the habit of deferring difficult work until a later time, you will miss opportunities that could have made you great. It was Babe Ruth in the movie Sandlot that said, 'Everybody gets one chance to do something great. Most people never take that chance, either because they are too scared, or they do not recognize it when it spits on their shoes'.

Procrastination delays you from reaching your goals. Irrespective of the efforts you put into self-discovery and goal setting, if you do not overcome procrastination, you will never accomplish your desires. You will only remain in the realm of talkers and fail to take the leap to the domain of achievers. If realising your goals is supposed to make you happy and fulfilled, it means that procrastination will likely do the opposite.

Procrastination could ruin your career. If you consistently defer work till the last minute, you may lose your job. No employer wants to retain an employee that fails to consistently meet deadlines. Sooner or later, your employer will start looking for a replacement for you. On the other hand, if you are an entrepreneur, and customers cannot trust you to deliver as, and when due, you will soon be out of business.

When you experience any of the downsides of procrastination that have been discussed above, you will have lower self-esteem and confidence. You will begin to doubt your ability to get work done. Also, you can damage your reputation. Ultimately, you can become depressed. However, you do not have to wait till you experience these downsides before you begin to strive for victory over procrastination.

> 'The really happy people are those who have broken the chains of procrastination, those who find satisfaction in doing the job at hand. They're full of eagerness, zest, productivity. You can be, too'.
>
> *Norman Vincent Peale*

DAY 29

TOPIC: COMMON REASONS WHY PEOPLE PROCRASTINATE

I believe that a solid knowledge of the common reasons why people procrastinate will help you in the fight against procrastination. Some of them are discussed below.

Goals that are not well set. The propensity to procrastinate is heightened when goals are vague. Conversely, when goals are clear, specific and well-defined, the likelihood of procrastination is very low. For example, if your goal is to become wealthy, the possibility that you will procrastinate work is high because that goal is too vague. However, if you have a specific aim of increasing your savings by $2500 at the end of 2 months, you will get more serious with work and spend less, so you can increase your savings. Also, if you have a desire to lose weight, you will likely procrastinate working out. However, if you set a target to visit the gym every Tuesday, Thursday and Saturday, you will most likely act on your goal. If you set goals without designing appropriate action plans, you increase your chances of procrastination.

Focus on future options. Some people procrastinate because they think that they will have a better opportunity in the future. For example, an individual who wants to develop a singing voice might avoid rehearsing at home because he hopes he would sign up with a music school in the future. Even though starting at home would not prevent them from switching to a more serious voice training plan in the future, this individual will still prefer to wait until a later time. Also, some people procrastinate because they are optimistic that they will complete the job in the future. What they fail to realise is that the only moment they can control is now, no one can control tomorrow. Therefore, the most challenging and essential activities should be done now, while others can be done later. For example, instead of sleeping now and doing your project later, do your project now and sleep later.

Perfectionism. Several people put aside work because they think they are not well-equipped enough to handle it now. To start with, let me say that it is good to wait for the right moment to get work done. Yet it is equally important to realise that you cannot do 'perfect' work. What I mean is that if you pick up a job you did 2 or 3 years ago, you will still discover errors. The truth is that as you grow in knowledge, you will find that the works you did before could use improvement. Therefore, if you wait to acquire all the knowledge there is before solving a problem, you will never get anything done. It is better to do your work today to the best of your ability than wait for tomorrow when you think you will have improved your skills. This is not to encourage mediocrity, but to say that being diligent about your work will give you more time to go over it again before submission. This gives you more chances of attaining excellence.

Closely associated with perfectionism is the fear of negative feedback. Some people avoid doing things that will bring them under the spotlight because they are afraid of public scrutiny. Many times, these fears are exaggerated. You must learn to accept evaluations and feedbacks. Do what is required of you, receive feedback, learn, and keep growing. I am yet to read the story of any successful person who got everything right during their first attempt, or who never failed.

There are other reasons why people procrastinate. I want to encourage you to find yours.

> 'Perhaps the most valuable result of education is the ability to make yourself do the thing you have to do, when it ought to be done, whether you like it or not'.
>
> *Thomas Huxley*

DAY 30

SUB-THEME: OVERCOME PROCRASTINATION

TOPIC: HOW TO CONQUER PROCRASTINATION

The first step to overcome procrastination is willingness. When I introduced this sub-theme, I encouraged you to meditate and discover some of the impacts that procrastination had on you in the past. The aim of that instruction was to stir up your heart to become willing to overcome it. Bad habits generally require firm decisiveness and commitment to change them. I am optimistic that by now you have realised that procrastination is not suitable for you and that you will give whatever it takes to avoid it.

The next step to take is to set specific goals followed by action plans. Previously in this book, we have discussed how to set goals and action plans. Please, refer back to them. Make sure that your goals are broken down into bits that you will accomplish every day. Ensure that each bit is achievable within a short time during the day. For example, if you are a beginner, do not design an action plan to work out for 2 hours a day. If you do this, you will most likely procrastinate and eventually stop doing the workout. You can start with 20 minutes for three days in a week, and grow from there. A famous maxim says that 'slow and steady wins the race'.

Furthermore, you have to realise that the only perfect time to do whatever you want to do is now. There is no other time than now. If you do not do it now, you will never get it done. You must learn to do things whether you feel like it or not. Also, you can use positive affirmations to tune in to your emotions to help you do what is required of you. Every successful person does what is required of them, not just what they feel like doing. If you want to join them, you have to learn to do what is necessary whether you feel like it or not.

Do not be afraid of mistakes. It was Theodore Roosevelt, the 26th president of the United States of America, who said, 'In a moment of decision, the best thing you can do is the right thing to do, the next best thing is the wrong thing, and the worst thing you can do is nothing'. Imagine a child who procrastinates walking because he is afraid to make mistakes. That child will never walk. Oftentimes, we learn better ways of doing things when we make mistakes, and the good news is that most errors can be fixed. You do not have to be afraid, just do what you have to do according to the best of your ability and at the time you are supposed to get it done.

Reduce distractions. It is wise to remove objects that lure you into procrastinating from within your reach. For example, if you always end up watching movies when you ought to read, it is beneficial to keep your phones and computers away from you when it is time to read. Also, you may need to look for comfortable locations where you can get things done. However, never allow location to become an excuse for why you will not achieve your daily targets. Whatever the conditions, ensure that you do what you can all the time.

Finally, you need to keep yourself accountable. You need to create a community of trusted friends and family members to whom you can report your progress on a regular basis. This will help you do what you have to do at the right time. For example, I am in the industry of public speaking, and I have vowed to myself to practice the art of speaking for a certain number of hours a day. Likewise, my great friend Malik Kaddu is in the movie industry, as an actor, has vowed to himself that he will spend a certain number of hours in the day working on different speaking accents and his overall acting skills. We keep ourselves accountable by simply asking this question, 'Have you done your hours?' Whenever we speak over the phone or meet in person. That simple question always keeps us accountable because neither of us wants to answer that question by saying 'No'. It keeps us both on our toes. Other ways to keep yourself accountable include making to-do lists or using your phone and calendar as reminders.

> 'Success is not obtained overnight. It comes in instalments; you get a little bit today, a little bit tomorrow until the whole package is given out. The day you procrastinate, you lose that day's success'.
>
> *Israelmore Ayivor*

DAY 31

SUB-THEME: **PLAN YOUR ENVIRONMENT**

TOPIC: **INTRODUCTION**

An old Spanish proverb says that 'Show me your friend, and I will tell you who you are'. Another popular adage says, 'The kind of friends you choose often determine your success in life'. I want to tell you today that the people around you can significantly influence the realisation of your goals, whether positively or negatively.

There was a farmer long ago who, one day, went to his farm and saw an eaglet in a nest, but the mother was not present. He took the eaglet home and kept it in the same cage with his chickens. Basically, the young eaglet grew to maturity amidst chickens. As such, every time the farmer let the animals out of the cage, they would all peck things from the ground, just the way chickens do. This eaglet never knew that it had the capacity to soar to unimaginable heights. It only learnt to do what the chickens did.

One day, a mature eagle sat on a tree near the farmer's residence, and watched the chickens peck food from the ground. Suddenly, something caught its attention. It saw an eagle among the chickens. The matured eagle noticed that the bird was different from the others and looked like itself. It then made a loud shrieking sound, and all the animals fled, including the young eagle. The farmer came out and put the animals back in the cage.

The next day, around the same time when the animals were let out of the cage, the mature eagle came again and sat by in the tree. This time, the young eagle started taking note of the adult eagle. It noticed that they looked alike. When the mature eagle made a shrieking sound, the young eagle refused to run with the other chickens. This was when the mature eagle spread its wings, and the young eagle also tried to do the same. It found that it could do it. The adult eagle then flew a bit, and the young eagle followed. The mature eagle then took the young eagle away and taught it how to soar.

Several people are like the young eagle; they can soar, but are busy pecking food on the ground because of the people around them. They are not surrounded by people who can challenge them; therefore, they do not grow more than the average. Several studies have shown that the nature of the people around an individual can affect a person's behaviour. Your friends determine how you think, make decisions, and ultimately, your self-esteem.

Have you ever caught yourself using a favourite phrase of one of your friends? Or have you discovered that you find it challenging to eat a meal that your parents do not like? This is a simple fact that shows that the people in our surroundings influence us to a significant extent.

The sad reality is that even though people in our environment are crucial to the realisation of our goals, we do not spend enough time thinking through our decisions before selecting our friends. Several people will carefully choose an outfit for an occasion then pay attention to the critical examination of the people they call friends.

In the next few days, we will dig deeper into how the people around you have affected the pursuit of your goals. However, for a start, I want you to take some time out to meditate on how your friends have been helping or preventing you from accomplishing your dreams. List five of your top friends, and list five of your goals. Determine how each of these friends has influenced the pursuit and realisation of those goals.

'You are the average of the five people you spend the most time with'.

Jim Rohn

DAY 32

TOPIC: **TYPES OF FRIENDS**

Aristotle, one of the most influential ancient Greek philosophers and scientists, who is also one of the brightest intellectual figures of western history, attached great importance to the concept of friendship. In his opinion, friends are valuable possessions, and they can help you achieve an extraordinary life. It was Aristotle who said, 'Without friends, no one would want to live, even if they had all other worldly things'.

Aristotle described three primary types of friends that each person will meet on their life journey. Today, we will review these types of friends, discovering more detail. More importantly, we will classify our friends into these three categories and see how much help or damage they have done to us.

The first type of friendship identified by Aristotle is the **self-interested friendship.** These are friends who use others only to benefit themselves. These people are not interested in the growth and development of their friends; what they care about is personal gain. They only support their friends if the course is promising. These types of friends can get others to do things for them through flattery and manipulation. Once they think an individual is no longer useful, they leave the friendship.

The second type of friendship acknowledged by Aristotle is the **pleasure-friendship.** These types of friends do not care about goals, dreams, and excellence, all they want is to have fun. They live a pointless, empty life. Once you begin to talk about serious matters, they lose interest. However, when you talk about something fun, having a good time, and partying, they take the front row. If they are wealthy, they cannot give you money to support your dreams or passion, but they can provide you with cash to throw a huge party. If they are not wealthy, they will stick around as long as you satisfy their cravings. Once you stop, they leave the friendship.

The last type of friendship identified by Aristotle is the **perfect friendship.** Those who desire to be great commit themselves to spending time with friends who share similar traits. This kind of friendship transcends pleasure and utility. They love you for who you are, support your dreams, goals and passions, and encourage you to be a better person. Ideal friends serve as your accountability partners. They motivate you to achieve your dreams. They not only inspire you to be better through their words, but also through their actions—they are also growing to become better people. Life becomes better when you keep these kinds of friends around.

Other types of friends that an individual could keep include **friends by history.** These are people that you have known for long. It may be that you grew up together in the same neighbourhood, attended the same school, or social gatherings. They may or may not have any real influence on you at the moment, but you need to pay attention to them too.

Another type of friends are the **friends by proximity.** These are friends that come into your life because of your relationship with someone else. They could be your friends' friends, your siblings' friends, the children of your parents' friends, and so forth.

The last type of friends we will discuss today are the **friends by context.** These are people that come into your life because of something you are doing. Perhaps both of you have the same passion or goal, or you do something together every day. Your colleagues at work or school fall into this category.

I want you to analyse your friends based on the different categories we have discussed. How did they come into your life? What influence do they have on you? We will discuss the types of friends that you need in your life tomorrow.

> 'Associate only with positive, focused people whom you can learn from and who will not drain your valuable energy with uninspiring attitudes. By developing relationships with those committed to constant improvement and the pursuit of the best that life has to offer, you will have plenty of company on your path to the top of whatever mountain you seek to climb'.
>
> *Robin Sharma*

DAY 33

TOPIC: THE ANATOMY OF THE FRIENDS YOU NEED TO ACHIEVE GREATNESS

Yesterday, we discussed the types of friends that people generally have. I believe that you now know the types of friends that you have. Today, I want to tell you about the characteristics of the friends that will drive you to achieve greatness. I am optimistic that by the end of today's reading, you will know exactly which of your current friends you need to keep, and what to look out for in the new friends that you will make. Let us get into it.

Loyalty. Great people keep loyal friends. Friends that will stay with you even when you make mistakes, people who will help you stay sane, individuals who do not judge, condemn, or destructively criticise you. People who will support your dreams both in your presence and absence. Friends who will defend you in public but rebuke you in secret. You need loyal friends.

Honesty. Some people are blindly loyal. They support whatever you do, whether it is right or wrong. They do not correct you; these types of friends cannot push you to greatness. You need honest people who can tell you their heartfelt opinions about things without fear or favour. You need people who are not battling with insecurity issues to the point that they cannot tell the truth. You need people who can look you in the face and tell you that you have not done well. You do not need people that will flatter or manipulate you. You need honest friends.

Ability to mentor. You need friends who have succeeded in life, and have the requisite to mentor you to greatness. These mentors do not have to share the same profession with you, they do not need to have the same goals and passions as you, but they must have succeeded in their endeavours to the point that they can inspire you to succeed as well. You must ensure that you are not the brightest person in your circle of friends. You need people who can motivate you through their lives, people who have the connections you need. You need a mentor.

Open to learning. While it is true that you should not be the brightest person in your circle of friends, you also should not be the 'dullest'. There should be some of your friends that are looking up to you for guidance and direction. In other words, you must have mentees. Every great person has people whom they look up to and people who look up to them. One of the most significant investments anyone can make is to invest in people. Therefore, it is necessary to have people who think they can learn one or more things from you in your circle of friends.

An adventurous mindset. It was George Addair, the founder of Omega Vector, who said, 'Everything you have ever wanted is on the other side of fear'. Your dreams and goals will sometimes look impossible and you will need friends with an adventurous mindset to encourage you to pursue them regardless the cost. These types of friends are willing to try something new and also motivate others to achieve new things. They never believe in impossibility, and they do not give up easily. My trusted confidant, Shenelle Darko employs this trait, she has always believed in me and we constantly push each other towards greatness. This is because our adventurous mindset rubs off each other. Other qualities that your friends must possess include diligence, foresight, empathy, dedication, and perseverance, among others. If you have friends who possess these qualities, your journey to greatness will be smoother.

> 'Walk with the dreamers, the believers, the courageous, the cheerful, the planners, the doers, the successful people with their heads in the clouds and their feet on the ground.'
>
> Wilfred Peterson

DAY 34

SUB-THEME: **PLAN YOUR ENVIRONMENT**

TOPIC: **BENEFITS OF HAVING THE RIGHT PEOPLE AROUND YOU**

Studies have revealed that having the right people around can help individuals achieve significant success in their finances, career, and other aspects of life. Discussed below are some of the specific impacts that inspiring people can exert on an individual's pursuit of greatness.

Good people inspire you to be diligent. A group of researchers from the HSE Center for Institutional Studies conducted a survey in 2015. They studied the academic performance of over 100 Russian university students. The results of the study revealed that students, who were friends, had similar performance. Also, between 2013 and 2014, a study was conducted on students' social network data. The findings of the study revealed that although most students do not choose their friends primarily because of academic performance, those who made friends with successful students managed to improve their grades. On the other hand, those who made friends with students who were not performing well in their studies experienced a drop in their grades. These studies prove to us that having the right people around can motivate you to work harder than you are doing at the moment. If you want to achieve excellence, you cannot leave the choice of your friends to chance. You must carefully choose friends who are high achievers in their respective fields.

Good people improve your self-control. The results of several studies conducted by psychology students at Duke University show that individuals with low self-control can resist negative temptations better when they keep strong-willed friends around them. Since self-control is crucial to achieving goals, having good people around can boost your own self-control, and in turn, increase your chances of success. Whether you are considering spending your savings for the month, or you are thinking of giving up on your dreams, spending time with disciplined people can help you stay on the right track.

Good people help you stay healthier. A group of researchers from Concordia University in Canada conducted a study on some international students who moved to Montreal. The reason for selecting these students was that they experienced a significant social transition after changing cities. The subjects were studied for five months. During this period, the subjects were asked if they felt lonely or not, and their heart rate fluctuations were tracked as well. The findings of the study revealed that the participants who did not make new friends in the new city and remained isolated had decreased heart rate variability. This means that they were more susceptible to cardiac diseases. However, the participants who made new friends in the new city and developed strong social networks had increased heart variability. This means that they were not susceptible to cardiac diseases and were generally healthier than the participants in the first group. I believe you must have heard that 'health is wealth'. The only goal of someone who is not healthy is how to get off the sickbed. In other words, there is nothing like pursuing greatness when you are sick. Therefore, you must stay healthy to achieve excellence. To do this, you must keep good people around you, because having a robust social network can improve your overall health.

Keeping good people around has other benefits for greatness. However, I am optimistic that the few reasons discussed above are sufficient to motivate you to choose your friends more deliberately.

> 'Look around you at the people you spend the most time with and realise that your life can't rise any higher than your friendships'.
>
> *Mandy Hale*

DAY 35

SUB-THEME: PLAN YOUR ENVIRONMENT

TOPIC: TOXIC PEOPLE

For the past few days, we have focused on the influence good people can have on the accomplishment of our dreams, aspirations, and goals. For the next few days, we will look at the impact of toxic people on our pursuit of greatness. When we talk about harmful or toxic people, it may not be that the people are bad in themselves. However, they do possess qualities that hinder you from achieving your dreams.

To remove toxic people from your life, you first need to know who they are. Toxic people are manipulators, great actors, and skilled liars. Every time you hang out with them, you feel negative, emotionally drained, and exhausted. They demotivate you, cast aspersions on the possibility of achieving your goals, talk you down, and remind you of the number of times you have failed. They never believe that you can attain greatness.

Toxic people have insecurity issues. As such, they need to make others feel pain to make themselves feel good. They never apologise for the wrong things that they do, instead, they play the blame game. Some toxic people might have been helpful in the past because you depended on them. The only reason they have become toxic is because you have begun to find a life for yourself. They want you to always rely on them for financial support, counsel, or other things. They want to control how far you can go in life and as such, they want to be part of your dreams and aspirations. They never desire for you to grow to a point where you can make decisions by yourself.

While some toxic people may not be aware of the negative influence that they have on people, others seem to derive some form of joy and satisfaction in driving the ones around them crazy. Toxic people make you doubt your ability to achieve your goals. While some of them do this because they do not want you to become more successful than they are, others do it because they genuinely want you to be safe.

A perfect example is one of my older sisters, who wanted to put her eldest daughter through private school. The financial hurdles that characterised the environment we grew up in made attending private school an almost impossible endeavour. As a second-generation Ghanaian growing up in Amsterdam and London, depending on the government for benefits has always been the safest way for us to make it through life—this meant attending public school. Therefore, the thought and audacity to try and push your child to attend a private school goes against the status quo. Many of my older sister's friends started to discourage her from pursuing her dream of providing private education for her children.

I was on the phone with my sister many times to encourage her. Usually, I would ask her 'Why do you even entertain such people? They clearly do not want the best for you or your daughter. Why do you still pick up their phone call?' and I reminded her that 'They want you to do well but not better than them. Sis, such people cannot be your friends, because a true friend will always push you towards excellence'. I kept on encouraging her that she should not think about the money, but rather about the benefits it could provide for her child.

Today, against the status quo, my niece is attending a private school. My sister always credits me as one of the reasons why she was able to put her child in private school, because of the support system and encouragement I provided for her when her friends were toxic.

> 'Some of the most poisonous people come disguised
> as friends and family.'
>
> *Anonymous*

DAY 36

TOPIC: **HOW TO DEAL WITH TOXIC PEOPLE**

Dealing with toxic people can be quite challenging. Still, by following the steps that will be discussed below, you should find it relatively easier to manage the fallouts from the toxic behaviours of others.

Speak up. Toxic people, sometimes use emotional blackmail to keep their subjects perceptually stuck with their toxicity. In situations like these, it may feel like it is easier to do what they want than bear their emotional torture. However, I want you to know that if you continue to give in to their demands for short-term ease, you are directly inflicting long-term pain on yourself. Most toxic people will not change if you keep pretending that you are okay with their toxic behaviour. You need to speak up. You need to decide that you will no longer have any of their toxic attitudes, stop tiptoeing around them, and desist from making special pardons for their sustained pugnaciousness.

When you speak up about someone's toxic behaviour, be careful to stay on the issue. Do not attack the person. Practice assertive communication: speak clearly about what they have done and how it affected you, and allow them to talk too. Also, ensure that you do not make general claims like 'I noticed you do not like me,' or 'I think you do not want me to achieve my dreams'. Be specific, and deal with issues as they arise. For instance, if you are talking to someone and the person seems to be angry, probably because he or she is jealous, you could say, 'I feel like you're getting angry. Is something upsetting you?'

When you challenge a person's attitude directly, it could disarm the person if indeed the individual was not aware of the negative impacts of his or her attitude. Even if the person denies your observation, you have successfully made the person aware that you will not condone such attitudes. If you refuse to speak up about someone's toxic behaviour, you are only indirectly encouraging them to continue behaving in such manner.

Some toxic people might resort to anger, and deliberately twist what you have said. Do not apologise. Instead, repeat what you have stated clearly, and explain to them that you do not mean what they have thought. If they leave in annoyance, let them be. Sooner or later, when they realise that their antics did not work, and will find a way to come back. This time, however, they are aware that they cannot control you by emotional blackmail anymore.

Do not allow them to make you the reason for their behaviour. Toxic people will try to make you believe and feel like you did something wrong that warranted their toxic reactions. This antic works because, generally, we feel guilty when other people make us feel like we are responsible for their woes. However, you must resolve not to allow this to happen to you. Toxic people do not display toxic behaviours because you did something wrong. Instead, they show toxicity because they are toxic. It is not about you, it is about who they are. If you pay attention, you will discover that most toxic people do not display toxicity towards you alone, they do it to others as well. Therefore, do not let them make you feel like you are the reason why they are toxic.

Tomorrow, we will continue learning about how to deal with toxic people.

'Letting toxic People Go is Not an Act of Cruelty. It's an Act of Self-Care.'

Anonymous

DAY 37

TOPIC: HOW TO DEAL WITH TOXIC PEOPLE 2

Yesterday, we learnt some of the ways to deal with toxic people. I emphasised speaking up and refusing to allow them to make you feel like you are the reason why they are toxic. Let us consider some additional methods below.

Practise compassion. Sometimes, you need to be sympathetic towards people who exhibit toxicity, because some of them are genuinely distressed. However, you need to develop the ability to separate their problems from their toxicity. You cannot help a person if you continually excuse their toxic behaviours because they have issues. You have to let them know that you do not tolerate such actions. If you regularly pardon them, you will only help them become more comfortable with projecting their insecurities on to you. You can only practice true compassion when you set boundaries. Let the toxic person know where you draw the line. Never start what you are not willing to finish. Overlooking too many toxic behaviours is not practical or healthy for you in the long term. Therefore, do not start it at all.

Create time for yourself. If you are dealing with a 'necessary' toxic person, that is, a toxic person that you cannot readily avoid, you need to consistently make time out for yourself so that you can rest and build up your strength. It can be challenging to get negative feelings out of your mind when you spend time with toxic people, and if you are not careful, you too can become toxic as a result of the toxicity that is displayed towards you. To avoid this, you need to create time for yourself to be alone. You deserve to have the opportunity to think about your dreams and goals without anyone interrupting you with toxicity. If possible, go on vacation and move away from everything that reminds you of toxicity.

Move on without them. Once you have realised that a person is toxic, and you do not seem to be able to help that person, you need to ask yourself if you really need them in your life. When you remove toxic people from your life, you will have some relief. You need to be strong to say enough is enough! Removing toxic people from your close circle does not mean you are annoyed or that you are keeping grudges. It only means that you care about your well-being. The parties in true friendship must both give and take. However, when you are the only one giving, and they are always taking, then you may need to let them go. Even though letting toxic people go should be the last resort, after all else has failed, it is the only viable option. When you move on without them, they will, most likely, resolve to emotional blackmail, but grow beyond that.

You must deal with toxic people in your life, otherwise, all your efforts at achieving your dreams will be sabotaged.

'Stop letting people who do so little for you control
so much of your mind, feelings, and emotions.'

Will Smith

DAY 38

The task of networking with new people can be daunting, yet highly rewarding. When you surround yourself with the right people, you increase your chances of success. The single most important tip that can help you when you are networking is to seek people whose goals align with yours. The more divergent your friends' goals are from yours, the higher the chances that they will be toxic to your dreams. You must ensure that the friends you keep are people who are going in the same direction as you. For instance, let's imagine that you and a friend need to push a tray. You are pushing towards the north, while your friend is pushing towards the south. It is fairly obvious that you will sabotage each other's efforts, and you will consider each other as toxic, but the truth is that you both are only moving in different directions. However, if both of you push in the same direction, you will have a greater impact. Therefore, ensure that you do not just make friends for the fun of it, seek those that are moving in the same destination with you.

Do not be afraid. You may have heard stories about how other people had terrible times with the people they newly met, or you may have had a bad experience meeting a new person. I do not intend to tell you that this information is false. Instead, I want to encourage you to not be afraid. What you may not have taken into consideration is the fact that the person you are about to meet is also scared of the things that scare you. You must note that a large percentage of people worry about the impression they make when they meet a new person. Only a small proportion are aware that great relationships are not built on what someone does during one encounter, but on the values and principles by which people live.

Start small. You should start by considering people that are closely related to you in one way or the other. Ask for a meetup, discuss with them, and get to know their values and principles. You could also find out if there are cliques that you could join. Sometimes, a group of people with the same values and ethics form a circle of friends, and they motivate each other towards excellence. Identify such groups and join them. You can also use social networking platforms such as Facebook and WhatsApp groups, among others. If you are an entrepreneur, for example, there are different entrepreneurial groups that you can join on various social platforms, where you can make network with people who live by the same values and principles that guide your life.

Get to know the person. Do not allow temporary things to take over most of the time you spend with new people, get to know their values, goals, priorities, drives and motivations, completed projects, and so on. Also, do not hold back information about yourself from them. However, be careful not to reveal sensitive information about yourself or your family members to new people.

Do not pretend to be who you are not to attract new friends. Let the people you meet know the exact person with whom they are dealing. For example, if you are an extrovert, but you pretend to be an introvert when you meet a new person, what happens when you become their companion? Will you keep pretending all your life? Just be real. People who want to be your associate will stick around, and anyone who does not want to be your friend can go. Remember, you do not need toxic people in your life; you need people who appreciate you for who you are, and inspire you to greatness.

'Do not be afraid of new beginnings. Do not shy away from new people, new energy, new surroundings. Embrace new chances at happiness'.

Billy Chapata

DAY 39

....

SUB-THEME: HELP OTHERS

....

TOPIC: INTRODUCTION

A Chinese proverb says, 'If you want happiness for an hour, take a nap. If you want happiness for a day, go fishing. If you want happiness for a year, inherit a fortune. If you want happiness for a lifetime, help somebody'. Helping others is, without a doubt, the quickest way to achieve success. Brian Tracy says, 'Successful people are always looking for opportunities to help others. Unsuccessful people are always asking, "What is in it for me?"' The truth is that the greatest success you will ever experience will come from helping others achieve their dreams.

Some people think that rich people became wealthy by being brutal and ruthless, therefore, they believe that to be rich, you have to be self-centred. However, Jack Ma, the CEO of Alibaba disagrees with that school of thought. He admits that the key to his success was, and is, helping others. It is practically impossible to achieve success without networking with others.

In 1903, when Henry Ford was about 40 years old, he founded Ford Motor Co. At that time, only the rich could afford 'horseless carriages'. Ford had a consuming passion for helping people solve their transportation problems. He captured this desire beautifully when he said, 'I will build a motor car for the great multitude, it will be so low in price that no man will be unable to own one'. This desire to help others did not only result in the production of the first dependable and reasonably priced 'automobile for the masses,' but it also sparked a revolution in the automobile industry.

J. Van Andel and Rich DeVoss started their career selling vitamins for a multi-level marketing company. However, they also had a desire to help others. Therefore, they came up with the idea of manufacturing a low-cost, biodegradable, all-purpose soap that could serve different purposes in an average household, and could be marketed by others for a profit. They worked with a chemist and created the product called 'Liquid Organic Cleanser'. The production of the cleanser led to the creation of Amway Corporation in Ada, Michigan. Today, this corporation has several household products sold worldwide including the United States, Asia, Europe, Canada and the South Pacific. J. Van Andel and Rich DeVoss both became one the wealthiest people in the world.

I can go on and on to give examples of people that became wealthy by having a desire to help others, and you will discover that most of the wealthiest people in the world had the desire to help others in their respective industries. Helping others is indeed the way to success. When you provide a solution to other people's problems, they open up their resources to you, and you become wealthier as a result.

'Doing nothing for others is the undoing of ourselves'.

Horace Mann

DAY 40

....

SUB-THEME: **HELP OTHERS**

....

TOPIC: **BENEFITS OF HELPING OTHERS**

Some of the benefits of helping others are discussed below.

You build your relationships. Humans are social by nature. As such, we usually feel the need to be connected to people, and by extension, the larger world. Helping others enables you to build new relationships, and improve on existing ones. In the quest to help others, you meet new people who also have this desire, and you bond faster because of your common goals. Furthermore, the things you learn while helping others will make you interact better with your family members, friends, and others around you.

You live longer. The results of several studies have revealed that the 'warm fuzzy' feeling that comes as a result of helping others has positive physiological effects that mostly pay off in the long term. Studies have shown that individuals who help others consistently live longer than those who are selfish and self-centred. Also, people who help others often report lower blood pressure, reduced stress, and greater happiness than those who do not.

You boost your self-esteem. When you see the result of the things you did to help others, you become more confident in yourself. For instance, do you think that Aliko Dangote, the richest man in Africa, whose products are in almost every home, would doubt himself anywhere? I certainly do not. Imagine the kind of confidence that will ooze from him if he enters any home. The results of several studies have revealed that self-confidence is a great predictor of success. Since helping others builds your self-esteem, it also increases your chances of achieving success in the long run.

If you are pondering whether to help others or not, I put it to you that it is your best chance at achieving your goals. When you attach your goals to the problems of the people around you, you will stop at nothing to solve it. You will always feel inspired and motivated in the pursuit of the realisation of those goals. Perhaps, this is why a lot of people give up on their goals, namely because the goals do not translate to any significant help for others. When your dreams transcend beyond you, you will experience heightened motivation.

'Only a life lived for others is a life worthwhile'.
Albert Einstein

DAY 41

SUB-THEME: HELP OTHERS

TOPIC: HOW TO HELP OTHERS

There are several ways through which you can help others. Some of them are discussed below.

Pay attention to others. When you start making an effort to remember the crucial details about others, such as their hobbies, children, and so on, you develop the ability to impact their lives positively. In business schools, you are taught to create a product only after carefully examining the needs of the people around you. It will be futile to give someone water if what they need is milk.

Share your network with others. You must be willing to help others meet people who can assist them in the pursuit of the realisation of their targets. When you discover an opportunity, talk to others about it. The more you connect people with those who can help them, the more you find that your network is expanding. Remind yourself that the road to success is a long route of networking. Therefore, as you network more, you increase your chances of meeting people who can help you achieve your desires too.

Inspire people. As you have the opportunity, you should encourage people who are discouraged. A couple of days ago, we discussed about keeping good friends around you, and I said that good friends would motivate you to achieve your dreams. However, if you want to have good friends, you must be a good friend too. Share your life story with others and help them learn how to make progress and achieve the success you have acquired. Do not be too quick to offer monetary help to others. Instead, show them how to make money. An adage says, 'Do not give me fish; rather, teach me how to fish'. Do not hoard knowledge from people.

Give honest feedback. Most people do not know how to give genuine feedback; therefore, they either flatter others or destructively criticise them. You must learn how to provide feedback about a person's work without attacking their personality. Generally, people often overlook the parts of a project that go well when they want to give their feedback. If you desire to help others, start by mentioning the things that the individual got right. Then, talk about what they did not get right, and offer them suggestions on how they can get it right, or refer them to materials or persons that can help them achieve excellence in that project.

'You have not lived today until you have done something for someone who can never repay you'.

John Bunyan

DAY 42

SUB-THEME: **HELP OTHERS**

TOPIC: **VOLUNTEERING**

Volunteering is a selfless activity where an individual or group of individuals offer to help another person or group of persons for free. It is one of the proven ways by which people help others, and make the world a better place to live. People often choose to volunteer for different reasons. For some, volunteering allows them to give back to the community. Others view it as a means of making a difference in the lives of those surrounding them. Volunteering, for some, provides a reliable means of skill development, and accumulation of relevant experience.

Kimberly Maul, an author at Idealist Careers, wrote the story of 23-year-old Jessica Thibodeaux, who obtained a paid position along with an enhanced view of her career path through volunteering. Jessica took a break from college because she could not afford to pay the tuition. Rather than sink into despair, she decided to put her efforts into volunteering.

She began by volunteering for *I'm Alive*, an online crisis chat network, where she received training, and got certified for works that relate to crisis line management. She moved from there to *Crisis Line* at Idealist Careers. She took the training and discovered that many of her recently acquired skills were also transferable to this new role. She was very active and exceptional in the class that her supervisor told her about a paid opportunity, and encouraged her to apply.

She applied and was employed, and then, she could sponsor herself again back to school, while working part-time. In Jessica's words, 'A lot of people forget about volunteering because it does require a lot of time and effort, and you could make money somewhere else. I just wanted to get the experience, and it ended up paying off more than I ever expected'.

Several famous and wealthy people have volunteered in different capacities to help others. Examples include Justin Bieber, who helps a lot of sick children. Oprah Winfrey, who created the Oprah Winfrey Leadership Academy Foundation in South Africa to support the education of young women and community growth. Ben Affleck, who founded the Eastern Congo Initiative to help victims of sexual violence, vulnerable children and give enhanced access to excellent healthcare services.

You do not have to be wealthy, like the people mentioned above before volunteering. You can participate in volunteering at whatever stage you are. All you need is compassion for others. Remind yourself that you build yourself up by helping others.

'The unselfish effort to bring cheer to others will
be the beginning of a happier life for ourselves'.
Helen Keller

DAY 43

TOPIC: **BENEFITS OF VOLUNTEERING**

Some of the benefits of participating in volunteering opportunities are discussed below.

Experience. When you start climbing the ladder of greatness, people will usually not believe in you enough to support you with their resources. Most employers, require prospective workers to have work experience before employing them. Volunteering allows you to garner experience while helping others. This in turn makes you more credible, because it tells your potential employers that you are excellent at time management, and you can complete tasks as and when due. Furthermore, your volunteering experience tells your potential helpers that you can work in collaboration with teams and persevere. Therefore, while volunteering helps make the world a better place, it also makes you credible for help to achieve your dreams.

Skill development. More often than not, volunteering opportunities will require that you develop new skills or build on the ones you already have. Either way, volunteering helps you become better at what you do. If you have a paid job, you might take up volunteering opportunities that will help you utilise the skills that you are not currently using on your job.

Network development. When you volunteer, you meet new people, as such, your network expands. You can never tell when and how you will need the help of any of these people later in life. Several people, like Jessica, have met helpers while volunteering. I am sure that you remember that you cannot succeed alone. You need others, and volunteering allows you to meet those others.

Shape your career goals. Volunteering can open you up to new pieces of information about your career. When you volunteer, you discover hidden details about yourself—your core values, your abilities, among others. When you take on a paid job, you are likely to constrain yourself to certain behaviours because you do not want to lose your job. But when you volunteer, you have the opportunity to know your true self in a non-threatening environment. This knowledge will help you shape your goals and targets.

Volunteering also helps thwart the effects of anxiety and stress. When you volunteer, you develop your social and relational skills. Also, volunteering makes you happy. It brings fun and excitement to your life.

'If our hopes of building a better and safer world are to become more than wishful thinking, we will need the engagement of volunteers more than ever'.

Kofi Annan

DAY 44

SUB-THEME: **HELP OTHERS**

TOPIC: **VOLUNTEERING OPPORTUNITIES**

There are several opportunities for volunteering. Some of them are discussed below.

Local schools. Many educators are stressed, overworked, and they need help. It has been discovered that schools work best when the community is involved. However, several community members, including parents, think that maintaining the school is someone else's responsibility. You can volunteer to read stories to students in elementary school, beautify the school environment, or monitor outdoor activities, among others. I have volunteered to speak to students in different schools, to motivate and inspire them with my story. I always feel a level of satisfaction and fulfilment taking up this role.

Senior centre. Several people dump their parents and grandparents in nursing homes, but these senior citizens need people to talk to, and with whom to build a connection. If you volunteer to spend an hour or two every week at a nursing home, you could be a great relief to those senior citizens. The thought of you coming to visit them could keep them alive much longer than they thought. Also, you could learn significant life lessons from these senior citizens.

Youth teams. Several organisations and groups host children and teenagers, but they need more coaches and assistants. You can volunteer to help with monitoring these children and teenagers. You can also start a youth group where you teach teenagers about the challenges of life and mentor them. When you mentor youths, you make the world immensely better.

Tutor students. Several students need help with some of their academic subjects. Aside from academics, you can help illiterate adults learn a language. This could make a lot of difference in their lives. You can gather students and teach them the use of technology and the internet. Also, you can volunteer to teach life skills like cooking or home repairs, among others.

Neighbourhood safety and hygiene. You can volunteer to serve as a guard to watch your neighbourhood when others sleep, depending on the prevailing circumstances. Also, you can team up with others to keep the community clean either by paying people to clean the neighbourhood, or by cleaning it yourself when you have spare time. When you participate in neighbourhood activities, you build a higher sense of community.

Hospitals. You can volunteer to man information booths, sit with patients, or work with children, in order to give the health workers more time to relax and tend to other patients.

There are several other aspects of life in which you can volunteer. Tomorrow, we will look into the essential aspects to take into consideration before selecting a volunteering opportunity.

'Volunteers do not necessarily have the time; they just have the heart'.

Elizabeth Andrew

DAY 45

TOPIC: **BASIC CONSIDERATIONS BEFORE SELECTING A VOLUNTEERING OPPORTUNITY**

There are several important factors to consider before accepting a volunteering opportunity. Some of them are discussed below.

Your skills and abilities. Different volunteering opportunities require different skills and talents; therefore, you must know what you have to offer before accepting to volunteer with an organisation. You must be familiar with the demands of the volunteering position before taking it up. In the first sub-theme of this book, we discussed self-awareness in detail. You can refer back to it for enlightenment reminder on how to become self-aware.

Your goals. Your goals should determine the volunteering opportunities you can take and those you cannot accommodate. If you are volunteering with an organisation, ensure that its vision and mission do not contradict your aspirations.

Availability. This is essential in volunteering. It is absolutely useless for you to take up a volunteering position without being available to do the work. You need to know the amount of time that an opportunity will require of you before taking it up. You need to ask questions and be sure you can accommodate the demands of that position before getting in. When determining your availability, you should consider both the time required and the location.

Do not be afraid to ask questions before taking up any volunteering opportunity. You should know if you will be required to take on additional training so you can fit into the position. You also need to know the people you will be working with, and to whom to report. You might consider starting small, probably with 30 minutes or an hour a week, and grow from there.

You must also know that volunteering does not end with large organisations. You can look out for your friends who are doing things that require your help. For example, if your friend is starting a business, and you are skilful in designing fliers, you can offer to create the business fliers for free. Find a way to support the people around you. Do not wait until they become great. Start with them, and grow with them.

> 'Volunteers do not get paid, not because they're worthless, but because they're priceless'.
>
> *Sherry Anderson*

DAY 46

TOPIC: HABITS OF EFFECTIVE VOLUNTEERS

To be successful at volunteering, there are certain habits that you must develop. Some of them are discussed below.

Consistency. This is the most important habit of any volunteer who seeks to be effective. You must make giving time a part of your schedule. If you desire to make an impact, you must be continually involved. You need to be deliberate about giving time to your volunteering work because if you are not careful, it can slip through the cracks. Make your volunteering service a priority by continually reminding yourself of the reasons why you decided to volunteer in the first place.

Flexibility. Sometimes, volunteering requires doing tasks that are not the most ideal. Effective volunteers know how to fit themselves in when they are needed to do something they do not particularly like. While it is true that you should volunteer for things that you enjoy, you must also know that there will be times that you may have to do something you do not really like, just to keep things in shape. If there is a shortage of human resources, you may need to do more than you signed up for. Successful volunteers know how to get comfortable with discomfort to attain the greater good.

Focus on the long-term impact. Effective volunteers are problem-solvers. They think about how to provide a solution to an organisation's problems. They do not focus on the temporary pain they need to go through while attempting to provide a solution. Instead, they prioritise the long-term effect of giving help. You will indeed be discouraged sometimes, but successful volunteers develop the habit of perseverance.

Seek out opportunities to grow. Some people volunteer to 'fulfil all righteousness'. However, effective volunteers take on leadership roles, and offer to help in more than one area. They do not wait to be called. They ask questions and offer themselves to work so they can improve their abilities. Also, they are open to feedback.

Finally, active volunteers find time to take care of themselves. They are aware that they need to be healthy to take care of others. They know when to 'slow down and fill their tanks'. Do not overwork yourself to the point that you have to give up volunteering in the future. Start at your level, and grow at your pace. You are not in competition with anyone.

> 'Service to others is the rent you pay for your room here on Earth.'.
>
> *Muhammad Ali*

DAY 47

SUB-THEME: **ASSESS AND ADJUST**

TOPIC: **INTRODUCTION**

It was Israelmore Ayivor, a writer, blogger, and speaker, who said, 'It is better to be slow and careful in the right direction than to be fast and careless on the wrong path. Be sure that you are on the right path before you begin to take steps'. Sometimes, you need to assess what you are doing in order to make sure that it is the right thing. Aside from this, you need to evaluate and adjust even the right things to make them better.

Mark Zuckerberg expressed interest in computer programming very early on in life. His parents got him a private tutor who trained him in computer programming. When he studied at Harvard, before he completed his sophomore year, he developed two programs: CourseMatch and FaceMash. The latter was shut down by the university's management board because they felt it was inappropriate. Zuckerberg, together with some of his friends, then created a social networking site that allowed Harvard University students to connect. He called it 'Facebook'.

Zuckerberg left Harvard before the completion of his studies to focus on growing his site. He worked so diligently that by the end of 2004, Facebook already had 1 million users. The truth is that Zuckerberg could have continued to develop Facebook just for the use of Harvard students, but he would not have been as successful as he is today. He assessed the situation, and discovered that many more people could benefit from Facebook. For this reason, he made necessary adjustments and opened up Facebook to other potential users. He started with students from other universities, and then proceeded to people from all walks of life. It comes as no surprise that as of the year 2020 Zuckerberg is the fourth richest man in the world, with a net worth of $86.5 billion.

Assessing and adjusting are essential to achieving excellence and greatness. Individuals who are resistant to making adjustments cannot attain greatness. If you have a creative idea, as soon as you start to implement it, you will realise that a lot of things need to be adjusted. You can never have all the answers to the question of greatness in the initial stages of pursuing a target. You can only assess and adapt as you go.

> 'It is not the strongest of the species that survives, nor the most intelligent that survives. It is the one that is most adaptable to change'.
>
> *Charles Darwin*

DAY 48

SUB-THEME: ASSESS AND ADJUST

TOPIC: ADVANTAGES OF ASSESSING AND ADJUSTING

There are several benefits derived from making the necessary changes, as and when due, in the pursuit of greatness. Some of them are discussed below.

You will achieve your dreams faster. People who dedicate time to constant evaluation and transformation often achieve their objectives quicker and on a grander scale than those who are resistant to change. The journey to greatness is laced with unpredictable circumstances that require making adjustments to cope with them.

You will lead better. If your goal is to be a leader, then, the ability to assess and adjust will be an added advantage for you. Individuals who develop the capacity to promptly assess situations and make the necessary changes excel as leaders. They earn their followers' respect and trust and achieve more than those who do not like to alter their strategies even in the face of challenging circumstances.

You will live happier. Individuals who are reluctant to change often become depressed and unsatisfied in life. Instead of adjusting their goals, strategies or action plans, they will keep complaining. Resilience is a crucial virtue that individuals who make adjustments possess and a basic recipe for success. It was Dean Becker, the president and CEO of Adaptive Learning Systems who said, 'More than education, more than experience, more than training, a person's level of resilience will determine who succeeds and who fails. That's true in the cancer ward, it's true in the Olympics, and it's true in the boardroom'.

You will put a stop to bad situations. Assessing and adjusting are the best ways to end unpleasant situations quickly. Irrespective of the cause of the adverse circumstance, an objective analysis and the willingness to make the necessary adjustments can put that situation behind you faster than anticipated. Also, when you assess and adjust, you open up yourself to more opportunities for attaining greatness.

The truth is that whether you cooperate with it or not, the change will happen. The only question will be whether you will benefit from those situations or not.

'insanity is doing the same thing over and over and expecting a different result'.

Albert Einstein

DAY 49

SUB-THEME: **ASSESS AND ADJUST**

TOPIC: **HOW TO ASSESS**

Some people are willing to make adjustments to their goals and action plans, but they do not know how to discover areas of their lives that require change. Today, I will show you some powerful tips that will help you understand if an area of your life requires adjustment.

Do not despise criticisms. To begin with, let me say that it is wrong to give negative feedback to others. However, if someone criticises you, whether destructively or constructively, do not focus on their method or approach, instead, concentrate on the substance of the feedback. When you allow people to give feedback about things that relate to you freely, your chances of discovering what needs to be changed are significantly increased. Do not put up any attitude that will make the people around you afraid to give you feedback, for therein lie the secrets to make your life better.

Meditate and Pray. It is easy to overlook a lot of things about your life when you are busy; however, if you dedicate time to daily meditation and prayers, you will become enlightened as to the areas of your life that you need to improve. You do not have to spend a fortune to create a place for meditation or prayer. All you need is a quiet place where you can think without distraction. When you meditate, you free your mind from all worries and anxieties, thereby, allowing it to think deep. Also when you spend time in prayer you allow God to take total control over your situation.

Seek knowledge. This is the best way to discover what needs to be changed. When you become more knowledgeable about something, you find out the downsides of what you have always done, and the advantages of doing something new. Therefore, you must commit yourself to a life of continual learning. The Bible even says in Hosea 4:6, that people are destroyed for lack of knowledge. Some of the ways to increase awareness include reading books, magazines and other inspirational materials, attending seminars and conferences, asking for insights from more knowledgeable people, just to name a few.

'You gotta make a change. You see the old way wasn›t working so it›s on us, to do what we gotta do to survive'.

Tupac Shakur

DAY 50

TOPIC: HOW TO ADJUST

There are three essential conditions for making necessary changes in your life. They are discussed below.

A burning desire. A lot of people only wish for change; they are not passionate about it. If you must make changes in your life, you need to create a burning desire. How are desires created? Find out the downsides of the old methods. When you discover the setbacks of the old ways of doing things, your desire to implement a new method will be heightened. Also, you need to find the benefits of doing something using a new method.

Be willing. After creating a desire for change, you need to develop the willingness to change. You must be aware that naturally, you loathe change. Therefore, you have to be intentional about creating a willingness for change. Have self-talk, and be ready and willing to see through the desire to implement a necessary change. Albert Einstein reminds us that, 'Insanity is doing the same thing over and over again, but expecting a different result'.

Be courageous. Making adjustments in your life requires courage. A lot of people fail at this point. They know that they need to implement change, they have the desire and are willing, but they lack the courage to implement those decisions. As soon as you have discovered a need for change in any area of your life, just go ahead and make the required adjustment. Remember that the more you delay, the more opportunities you miss.

Patience. You must realise that making adjustments to your life might not bring an immediate result. For example, if you have a business, and you discovered that you need to improve your product after conducting an objective assessment, your profits will likely not soar overnight after implementing these changes. It will take some time for the customers to become aware of the changes in the new product, test, and love it. There is greatness inside of you I am confident about that, just be patient your time will come when the world will celebrate you for your uniqueness.

> 'Every great dream begins with a dreamer. Always remember, you have within you the strength, the patience, and the passion to reach for the stars to change the world.'
>
> *Harriet Tubman*

FINAL WORDS

I am delighted that you have made it to the end of this book. I am optimistic that you have learned about the common denominator of high achievers and that you are ready to act accordingly. I am sure that you remember that reading through this book without taking action is as good as not reading it at all. My desire is that you will become great by applying the information available in this book.

It was John Barton, a British Anglican Priest, who said, 'You can never step into the same book twice, because you are different each time you read it'. Therefore, I encourage you to refer to this book again and again. The more you read it, the more you understand the principles discussed, and the more passionate you become about achieving greatness.

To my own people in the 'third world countries,' I assure you that by taking action based on the guidelines discussed in this book, you can become great and contribute your part towards removing the negative 'label' placed on you so that you can impact and become generational leaders.

I look forward to seeing you at the top!